At the Writing Desk

Werner Kofler

At the Writing Desk
Alpine Saga / Travelogue / Acts of Vengeance

Translated by Lauren K. Wolfe

DALKEY ARCHIVE PRESS

Originally published in German as
Am Schreibtisch: Alpensagen, Reisebilder, Racheakte
by Rowohlt Verlag, Reinbeck bei Hamburg, 1988

LIBRARY OF CONGRESS CATALOGING-IN-PUBLICATION DATA

Kofler, Werner, 1947-2011, author.
[Am Schreibtisch. English]
At the Writing Desk : Alpine Saga, Travelogue, Acts of Vengeance / By
Werner Kofler ; Translated by Lauren K. Wolfe. -- First edition.
pages cm
Summary: Installed behind his desk with notebook, ashtray, whiskey,
and "several typewriters of various calibers," Werner Kofler embarks on
a tour not through space but through literature, and through his abor-
tive attempts at producing a work he can call his own. "Art must destroy
reality," he trumpets, yet, in the spirit of his "beloved Beckett," each
failed attempt at the writing desk only drives the effort endlessly, angrily
on. The first English translation of a central figure in Austrian fiction,
At the Writing Desk is a battle cry against every cultural and literary
status quo -- Provided by publisher
Includes bibliographical references.
ISBN 978-1-62897-004-3 (pbk. : alk. paper)
I. Wolfe, Lauren K., translator. II. Title.

PT2671.O33A6913 2015
838'.91403--dc23

2015017789

BUNDESKANZLERAMT ═ ÖSTERREICH

Partially funded by the Illinois Arts Council, a state agency
The translation of this book was supported by the
Austrian Federal Ministry of Education, Arts and Culture

Dalkey Archive Press publications are, in part, made possible through
the support of the University of Houston-Victoria and its programs in
creative writing, publishing, and translation.

Dalkey Archive Press
Victoria, TX / McLean / London / Dublin
www.dalkeyarchive.com

Printed on permanent/durable acid-free paper

Translator's Introduction

Werner Kofler was born in 1947 in Carinthia, Austria—the scene of so many of the crimes that were to provoke the vituperative rage of a writer whose program for literature he was later to call a "fight against crime." Gert Jonke, a longtime friend of Kofler's and likewise compelled to literary exile in Vienna, describes the provincial, postwar atmosphere into which both men were "pitchforked" into this world as a kind of moral police state in which pleasure, art, and fantasy were met with bitter loathing and combatted by vehemently ideological poetry. Here, right-wing populists dominated the political stage, exploiting a nationalist sentiment befouled by the spirit of National Socialism on their march to power. Moral insipidity, artistic complaisance, political mendacity, and greed: these are not novel subjects for literature; but in Kofler's treatment they become the objects of a satire, of an aestheticized aggression so stringent, so disparaging, that even his associates admitted unease at the thought of having one of his "typewriters of various calibers" trained on them.

Of course, it's impossible to read of an enraged and despairing Austrian writer of the latter half of the twentieth century without Thomas Bernhard coming to mind. But if Bernhard was the alienated insider, Kofler was the great outsider, his less a literature of self-alienation and self-contempt than professional alienation and public contempt for the corruption around him that, rather than internalize, he raised to a level of unequivocal indictment. Perhaps it was inevitable, then, that he be "punished" for his unpalatable principles; Elfriede Jelinek, for one, alleged that the criminal negligence to which Kofler's works were subjected during his lifetime resulted from his own unyielding nonconformity; in her words, a crime had been committed against him by the literary scene, *das Verbrechen der Nichtbeachtung*, that of near total disregard. In the specific context of Austrian letters, so beset by scandal, this meant that Kofler, unlike Bernhard, was deprived of the very public outrage he sought. "Crime has a name and an address," he wrote, and from this dictum he "proceeded accordingly," calling on the perpetrators by name. He never dressed the objects of his derision in fictive clothing, never "thinly veiled" the persons or circumstances he sought to denounce. He was too shrewd for this, was hunting for bigger game—and this, paradoxically, made him both too specific to his own particular milieu to attract Bernhard's world renown, and too embarrassing within Austria to merit local success. Simply put, people were afraid of him.

Real persons appear in Kofler's fiction in places they may never have been, doing things they may never have done. For instance, the infamous Udo Proksch, the Austrian businessman who conspired to sink the *Lucona* in an attempt at insurance fraud, appears in *At the Writing Desk* as both an arms dealer in a mock detective thriller and an artist hired to recreate the Nazi extermination camps as a museum exhibit. Fictional characters too, those invented by other writers, make appearances in Kofler's work, satirizing the attitudes of actual public figures; or, as is the case in the present book, with the narrator of the chapter "In Treuchtlingen," new fictional characters are invented to infiltrate the worlds created by other writers. Even historical fact gets its proper mistreatment, in the aforementioned museum, which perversely documents a mythical inversion of the events of World War II, wherein the combined forces of Europe invade Germany. By strategic reinvention, by the distortion of reality "beyond recognition," by his "chronic insubordination to the dictates of the facts," Kofler's fiction is ultimately contending with reality, with the forms of cultural and social life that claim to represent the real.

In *At the Writing Desk*, a book that might be considered the most programmatic of Kofler's works, the media, literary, and political establishments are taken to task for the damages that their so-called realities have inflicted not only on art — *The Magic Flute* in the service of Nazi ideology, for instance, or the more contemporary demand for realism and naturalism in literature — but also on the very possibility of truth-telling. Kofler toggles back and forth between reality presented as fiction and fiction presented as reality, because it is the in-between separating them that tells of a more unsettling truth.

Kofler was a meticulous compiler, a conscientious archivist of his historical moment. He trawled the news, tabloid journalism in particular, feeding off the bottom in order to identify and excoriate the real bottom-feeders. He warped *Der Spiegel* into a funhouse mirror. His arch character sketches — or assassinations, rather — cheerfully lambaste criminal misconduct of every stripe, from sex-traffickers in the notorious St. Pauli district to the then American President Ronald Reagan. He embraced poor taste in his invective — in his words: the poorer the better! From the obscure and banal to the infamous and banal, Kofler's perhaps manic deployment of allusion, his "associative delirium" bewildered even his contemporary Austrian audience. Writing is "leaving traces," he wrote, leaving "clues, fingerprints behind, for the few who are left that can still read, and for as long as they still can." This is all the more true, necessarily, for his translators.

Werner Kofler died in December 2011, which is about the same time I began the work of translating this book. It was disheartening to be deprived of his collaboration, hunched over my own writing desk, attempting to follow the clues he left behind; more disheartening still to translate the words "my books don't get translated," and to be obliged to report to Kofler's new audience that only after an author is "dead and buried" can his books stand a chance at life.

But if that's the case — here's to life.

LAUREN K. WOLFE, 2014

At the Writing Desk

In front of me, the tour guide. He knows the way. If I lose my footing or my balance, he will save me; if I trip in the rope between us, he will safeguard me; and so that I don't, and so that he needn't—and since doing without a rope's not an option, I'm told—he climbs the path well ahead of me. If *he* were to fall or mean me ill, or seek to harm, I or all would be lost. Yes, I've hired him for my safety, I pay him well, I'm well secured, and I aim to make it to the top. I've paid him, so it's my orders he has to follow, and I follow him. At the moment, however, an inexplicable weakness seizes me, as it has once before while climbing Großelend—I was alone, the last time, and managed somehow to haul myself back down to the valley—my strength now suddenly gives way and I can't go on. Granted, it was well before dawn when we set out, we've been underway for a while now, I'm not all that adept at navigating this icy and treacherous terrain, off to our right ice ruts cut dizzying vertical paths in the rock face, but still I'm baffled, *bothered* in fact by this fatigue; little as I like to admit it, it's true. How about we call it a day? I call out to the tour guide. I think it's best we turn back now!—Whether we turn back, and when, is for ME to decide, as we agreed at the start, replies the guide with a brusqueness I hadn't anticipated when we set out. I can tell feigned fatigue from the real thing, you're not the first to plead fatigue at this point, the so-called Klammerkopf fatigue is what that is. Come on, now: onward and upward! I've got obligations to meet, responsibilities to bear, and frankly speaking, I need the money.—I have a little farm in the valley, the tour guide is forging ahead while I stagger behind, and with all that's happened of late, all that's been happening ... My father passed away this year: Woman, turn on the light! he says to my mother one night, I'm dying! and moments later he was dead ... And then there's my son, the tour guide continues, he got decent grades on his report card so I bought him a bicycle, he sped off in his joy to his great aunt's house high in the alpine meadow and on his way home he took a wrong turn, went careening down a bluff and was hurled, with unimaginable force, headlong into a mill; his busted skull did him in before the medevac helicopter even landed ... And a cousin of mine hanged himself shortly thereafter ... And not too long ago they discovered my brother, a rock collector, up on Hocharn peak, frozen to death, a piece of topaz the size of a nightstand in his ice-cold grip. A sudden plunge in temperature—the ranger had warned him, tried to prevent him—too late; three full days passed before they unearthed my brother's snowcapped body ... Ah, so many funerals in so short a time, seems I attract all manner of disaster, doesn't it ... But of course—the tour guide carries resolutely on, without the least concern for me, I hear his voice one minute as if from a great distance, then amplified the next by the rock face surrounding us, I've long since given up my lofty ambitions by now, but higher and higher still we climb—of course, *naturally*, I should say, we're simpleminded, they say we have a different relationship to death, you know, coming into being and passing away is an entirely natural affair, for the peasant, so they say, we see no deeper meaning in it ... Our kids get hurt, our kinfolk die, that's life, as the saying goes, no more appalling than a sheep struck by lightning or a cow with a broken foot! We don't *feel*, we go to church, and it's a long way down from here to the valley of the shadow, isn't it? We're devout, we light votive candles when it storms ...! And aren't we also *naturally* religious, haven't we always lived in fear of the almighty mountains, the mountain spirits? Yes, yes, ours *is* a nature religion, an ethnologist came here once and explained it: in our veneration of the virgin mother and the heavenly father something pagan, Celtic even, survives ... Ah, *appeasement*—the tour guide glances at me sideways as he says it—there's always an appeasement of one sort or another for our lot, devoted as we are, so devoted . . .

But all that's in the past now, that *was* the past! And now, we will not be appeased! We don't need any tourists any-more, any more *summer folk* out here rooting among the larch and pine, prowling around the turban lilies and col-umbine, as if they were the wonders of some ancient world! Agriculture, animal husbandry—no more! The tour guide is gasping. Rare pines, plunging waters, the renowned Tau-ern wolfbane—*boring*. We want jobs! We need industry, in-frastructure, glacial ski resorts, I tell you, cable cars, power plants! I'm telling you: power plants and more power plants, that's what we need, and that's what we'll get. The tour guide is shouting. Ah, all those tremendous masses of water cours-ing entirely unexploited into the Black Sea, trickling out into the Eastern Bloc . . . From glaciers and wellsprings into the valleys, from the valleys into the Drava, the Drava emptying into the Danube and the Danube into the Black Sea, it's in-credible. It's jobs we need! Plans were laid for the power plant I'm talking about back in 1938, and they still haven't built it, they've been too busy quibbling; if the original architects of the project ever got wind of that, well . . .! But the time has come: jobs, I say, *jobs*! The tour guide laughs. Have I even in-troduced myself? Yes? What name did I give you, then? To-bias Reiser, ethnomusicologist and master of the zither? Ha! That's a good one. Have to hand it to myself. Tobias Reiser. Not bad. So listen up, honorable alpinist, let's hear what you think of this: I am, in fact, Florian Köll, the man who raised a sleepy little backwater by the name of Windisch-Matrei to Europe-wide renown, you're looking at a veritable European *mayor*! And everything I told you about my little farm, my fa-ther's death—fraud! fiction! a rotten pack of lies! The rock face reverberates with the tour guide's laughter. My father en-joys excellent health, he's hale and hearty and has made quite a name for himself as a civil servant in the state government at Innsbruck; the Tyrolean governor Wallnöfer—a monument of a man, I tell you!—is a good friend of his. The son of mine who was killed in a bicycle accident? You, sir, have been taken for a ride! My son is far too fat to be riding a bicycle, which only goes to show how well he's doing. And, as you can imagine, my cousin didn't hang himself, nor did my brother die for the sake of a piece of semiprecious stone, that would have been stupid of him. No, both hold lucrative positions in the electric industry—in the operations division of the proposed power plant, to be exact—and are positively abounding in optimism. Now do you finally understand that it's too late, too late, *too late*! The tour guide is shrieking—his voice lashes my ears like a whip. We'll build a dam, the first of its kind, a work of art, no fewer than forty alpine pastures will disappear forever in the reservoir it'll create, glacial streams shall be despoiled of their pointless beauty so that their power may be harnessed to a beautiful purpose: the peaceful coexistence of economy and ecology, a *win-win compromise*! The kingfisher will come: *the kingfisher—native to our reservoir*, the kingfisher—sponsored by your electric company . . . No dam, no fowl—not bad, right? And we'll create jobs— oh, you have no idea! the tour guide shouts, breaking into laughter so infernal that I'm afraid it'll trigger an avalanche above us and we'll both be sent plummeting to our doom. Bullshit, this is *bullshit*, I want to call out but I can barely make a sound.

In front of me, the tour guide continues up over the ice. Although or even *because* he's aware of my condition—I'm not moving—he gives the rope an obstinate jerk and drags me onward, into the ferocious darkness descending overhead—or can it be descending over *my head alone*? Onward now, onward, toward progress, toward the light, I hear the tour guide shout as if from afar; is he laughing again, is he actually singing? A point of light appears in the distance, an Alpine shelter, the Prague Lodge, salvation! This thought has only just crossed my mind when the light blinks out and silence in turn descends over the darkness.

Behind me, the tourist. I'm keeping an eye on him, in every respect. To wit, he did hire me as his guide, but that only makes me wary and all the more suspicious. The more he talks himself up, tries to pass himself off as a *friend of the alpine peasant*, the greater my suspicion grows. This tourist, so I've gathered, is of that unpleasant variety of urbanites who fancy themselves more rustic than the rustics themselves, who all know better than we do, and who would like nothing more than to dream us back to the Middle Ages, for no better reason than that we might more neatly conform to the sketches they so enjoy making, unsolicited of course, of us and our homesteads! And what they insist on above all: no progress, no *relief*—as if there were no virtue in these things ... No high-profit monocultures, please, and no chemical fertilizers! No battery cages, no industrial hog farms, and no money. A paved road to facilitate logging? Certainly not! A milking machine? It's better for the cows if you do it by hand. There's been electric light in the valley for going on thirty years now? What a pity. A loan from the local credit union? That's a bit iffy! They come out here from the city only to regulate us or to ask pointless questions: Why aren't there shingles on that roof? Why isn't that oven in use? Where's the well-trodden dirt floor and the open hearth, and where's the iron kettle that ought to hang over it? Alpinists like this tourist here only come out to our neck of the woods in search of uselessness, luxury, the luxury of an unpurposed nature; which is not to say they don't also delight in our misery, in the tremendous self-reliance of the peasant, of which they'd like to persuade *us*, if only for the sake of preserving these medieval conditions for their own amusement.

I have to be careful. I won't go by Köll this time, or Reiser.

The tourist introduced himself to me as Thomas Bernhard, which I'm sure can't be his real name. He's trying to sound me out, that much is clear. It was a bit too nonchalant the way he tried steering our conversation around to that dead body out at Lake Zirbensee. See, the old country doctor allegedly let him in on the bizarre discovery of a corpse in the lake that's being built out into a reservoir—some hapless hunter, all kitted out, strapped to a stone slab as if laid out in state on the bottom of the lake ... The doctor's old and not quite right in the head anymore, I explained to the tourist. This guy's not getting a word out of me, certainly not about the circumstances surrounding some idiot out stalking deer who wound up falling into a lake and drowning (a man can still drown, after all, can he not?!)—not one word, especially not about some pigheaded idiot who refused to sell his pastures to the electric company so an access road to the construction site could be built. By all means, everyone's a bit pigheaded around here, but pigheadedly in opposition to other pigheads, not in opposition to the majority and to the public good—that we cannot have. Every other member of the community was prepared to sell, except for him; shall the majority allow itself to be tyrannized by a minority? This tourist has no need to know any of that. He's also revealed a disturbing interest in a long since overgrown burned-out spot down in the valley, and in the story of the night now over half a century ago that a building was torched and the land was scorched ... Why should he be concerned with the events of the night the Platterhof—that fine hotel, the finest!—went up in flames and burned to the ground? Why should he concern himself with that exceptionally hostile fire that lit up the night for miles around? Even I know next to nothing about it save what I've gleaned from those veiled references my father made, he swore me to secrecy, the heart keeps silent, that's what my father always said. It was all bound to come to an end eventually, the artists' colony, the half-naked women,

it, if you see what I'm getting at ... There's no real work anymore, no artistry, no craftsmanship, no manufacturing even, nothing but *jobs* ...!

The tourist has talked himself into quite the frenzy, and it's not a pretty sight. I haven't trusted him from day one. I can't always follow his arguments, but I'm the tour guide here, so he better watch out or I just might—

And yet, after a pause the tourist continues, and yet, just get this damn park built already! And yet, then again, don't! The instant that fencing goes up, the instant that roads make it *accessible*, the region is going to be overrun by an even greater and more offensive concentration of *ego*-tourists— he glances at me expectantly—than it's ever seen before. Oh, these flatland jackasses, for whom everything blurs into one *panorama*, one singular, marvelous, unparalleled *panorama*, who haven't even confidence enough to stray from the *Panorama Trail* or *Panorama Way*! How I hate them, with their fleece and flannel, polluting the place and scaring away the birds and wildlife with their nasty family gossip, stories of distant relations and ailments that they find it necessary to share in the woods, of all places ... But the mountain grouse isn't concerned with the Wernickes or the Würstleins of Bamberg, not with the Wernicke family drama nor the Würstlein saga; the lynx isn't asking for the latest updates on every Tom, Dick, or Harry; the badger isn't interested in the news breaking from anyone's urethra or large intestine; and were said news to have been leaked directly from the intestines of Frank Sinatra or the penis of the President of the United States, the badger still couldn't even be bothered to hope for the *worst*.—You ought to know, says the tourist—he talks and he talks, this is getting bizarre—you really ought to know that I consider America Public Enemy No. 1 ... But back to nature: My ancestors, you're not going to believe this, but they were farmers, hunters, gatherers, possibly even poachers ... It's from them that I've inherited my ability to stalk silently through the woods, and my keen eyesight, too, which isn't always the blessing it might seem ... Not too long ago at a trailside snack shop—it happened upon me quite by accident—I was forced to witness, you've got to picture it, a Franconian couple from Coburg with a Swabian and a Styrian couple sitting at a table embroiled in a furious contest of one-liners—I wish I could erase it from my mind! The lame witticisms, the inanity that came farting out of their mouths, the six of them sitting there shitting their lunatic laughter all over the table, all over their ham sandwiches and into their cups of buttermilk. It was too much. I had to get out of there. And people like these, in their ridiculous getups, have the nerve to laugh at me as I—in my sensible, dark green corduroy pants (and not a cheap pair, either!), with the walking stick I carved myself in hand—as I amble over the tree line, bare from the waist up, weather permitting, morons like these, with feathers in their felt hats, are laughing at me, in their short pants and flannel shirts, they go right on laughing ...

Of course I don't know what's more revolting, or who's more dangerous, more pernicious, I hear the tourist saying, the vulgar flatlander predator on the hunt for the rustic or our own chancellor surveying the land from atop Großvenediger ... Yes, the chancellor climbed Großvenediger—how tactless and irritating, incomparably so, unless of course the American ambassador who once climbed Großglockner is also in the running ...! (What a shameless human being this tourist is, I'd like to give him a piece of my mind, I think, and then I think better of it; this man needn't know that I was once in the service of that venerable Frau von Damm—Helene, a delightful woman, originally from Austria, she goes by Gürtler now.) What a revolting person, he curses, the new Director at the Hotel Sacher, and then out of nowhere he starts laughing, *There once was a Lady from Ulmerfeld*—oh, never mind, a good joke's just not coming to mind. Anyway, while the former ambassador atop Großglockner was a ridiculous spectacle, the former financier now current chancellor atop Großvenediger—that's just downright dangerous! I mean, picture it—the tourist just keeps talking, and it's clear he's not about to shut up anytime soon—you've got to picture it: this Social Democrat, looking like he's just stepped out of a Piz Buin sunscreen ad, climbing Großvenediger, trekking, just like we are, over snow and ice, in the largest glacial area of the eastern Alps, the Kristallwand looming before him in the early morning haze, the Schwarze Wand in the distance, he sees the plunging waters, the Tauern valleys and fertile meadows, forests of larch and pine, he takes it all in, and what's he thinking of? He's thinking of dams, retaining walls, pipelines, of explosive charges, chainsaws, bulldozers, helicopters, and cement mixers, of dust, dirt, din; from way up here, you can see it all, but all he sees is concrete. This chancellor looks upon perfection and thinks only of destruction, he walks through the woods nosing around for jobs, it's absurd! He and that stupid slogan of his that won him the election: *Make no promises, break no promises.* This big shot—lifting his *drivel* straight from Simmel, who, along with Fried (*reckless artistic nature*, indeed!), endorsed him in the run-up—this big shot is no blockhead, he's a *damhead!* The man has confused the national park with the national bank ... And he's barely descended Großvenediger before he ascends the podium of some labor union meeting and, to the hooting and hollering of the proles, starts heralding a new era for the reckless exploitation of hydropower: we will see it *done*, we will follow *through*, the majority hounded by a minority, no more! and never again!—all of which is met with the thoughtfully considered *frenetic* applause from the concrete workers' union. What's more, it was Hitler's idiots who'd planned to build a power plant here in the first place, and this chancellor is the one who decides he's going to make it a reality. *Native to our reservoir—the kingfisher!* the tourist shouts. The head of our government, so-called,

Matrei, not when it comes to jobs anyway, the mere prospect of jobs is enough to arouse the belligerent mountain men latent within. But, I'm sorry, here I've been regaling—oh, *boring* you, you say? Okay then, so I've been boring you—with my interpretation of the word *finish*, which evidently doesn't pertain. I've led you astray. See, I've overlooked something: Here, next to the note written in pen another note's been added in pencil—what awful handwriting, what a horrible mess!—*Attempts that break off*, and then, beside the names Rogner and Köll, *this—, that—, that—, who—*, and so on. The breaks he likely intends to fill in at some point with some manner of verbal assault, I'm sure he's got a whole litany in store. Yes, if this fictive first person of his claims he's able to see all the way to the Prague Lodge, which is a full day's hike from the Klammerkopf, what's to prevent me from seeing what's on his desk, this appalling disorder, why shouldn't I be able to decipher his terrible handwriting? So, the *finishing blow* will take place on the page, good to know—a lot gets written, little gets done. As a member of the Austrian People's Party, I view these attempts at slander with equanimity, whether or not he gets around to finishing them, and my friend Rogner will suffer no embarrassment as a consequence. A man like Rogner is extremely sensitive, particularly now that negotiations over the location and funding for his *History Land* project—the paying visitor as a participant in the process of phylogenetic human evolution, it's ingenious! The *adventure vacation* comes of age!—are being delayed due to bureaucratic spinelessness and petty misgivings. Rogner is by no means obliged to make the Villach valley home to his history of civilization, however, to erect his pile dwellings and his high medieval marketplace on either the new bend in the Drava or the wasteland that's been created as a result of the construction of the power plant. One false word and Rogner will give the nod to bidders from Florida or France, and the gentlemen of the domestic tourism industry will have no one but the author to thank for that. *No more,* and *never again,* is what Rogner would say; I'm packing up the project, I've had it patented, and I'm leaving, thanks to that man over there. I won't be publicly insulted, called a criminal, a backdrop painter, a historical *reconstructionist,* a fuckwit, and, what pains me most of all, a *Tomfool.* Even as a kid, just because my toys were elaborate and expensive, I was teased and called a Tomfool even though my name is really Robert; and when it would get to be too much, I'd take my remote-control race-car track or my battery-powered illuminated castle with me and go, I'd leave the playground, just like I'm leaving now, fare thee *poorly,* Gentlemen ... And with that, Rogner will parry the *finishing blow!* And our author will be powerless to stop it, literature doesn't make things happen, it can't prevent the construction of a recreational paradise or power plant, whose two hundred-meter high dam is destined to become a major tourist attraction in itself. Have I already told you about the thing with my brother-in-law? Well, my brother-in-law took a job in the electric industry, but that's not all, he also led the chancellor and a handful of his closest associates to the summit of Großvenediger, as their guide, just like I did with the tourist some pages ago. A private expedition for the chancellery, a staff outing as it were, the chancellor's a climbing fanatic, as everyone knows, although he's an avowed limestone climber, his mountaineering home is in the northeast, in the Salzkammergut. Now, my brother was very pleased with the chancellor, as a fellow alpinist as well as a chief executive who doesn't shy away from tough decisions, very pleased indeed. And this is in spite of the fact that they come from opposing political camps—in the fight against nature and the environment, consensus and resolve are imperatives of a higher order. My brother will conduct his business in a manner similar to the new transport minister. And my father is director of the water authority for the provincial government, a genuine *privy councilor,* and the governor is a friend of his.

en the bus one stop too far and now he has to walk all the way back, ha ha. In all likelihood he was thinking about his publisher, arguing with him in his mind, because of course they've had a falling out: the publisher wants him off the list, he's no good anymore—the author I mean. I don't know if it's the alcohol, the publisher told him straight to his face, or if it's laziness that's to blame, but all this stewing in your own juices, and all this *repetitiveness*—it's boring, there's nothing new here, no invention, nothing at all. He's been out for revenge ever since, our author. Yes, through the clear Alpine air I can see all the way to Berlin, into the offices of the press in question, the publisher's office opens onto the garden: after they finished talking business, the two of them chatted about Großvenediger and about pneumonia, which condition the publisher says he contracted there decades ago, which fact the author can hardly believe—about the pneumonia, that is, not Großvenediger. Now. The publisher is of course not the only one with whom this author—look at him schlepping along, ha! do you see?—has quarreled, there are very few colleagues with whom he hasn't had a falling out or whom he doesn't despise, a reason can always be found.—Look at him schlepping along, lost in thought, it would seem, turned inward, somehow absent yet on high alert—yes, look straight ahead, he's surveilling, he's eavesdropping on, in, all over everything. Say you run into him, you're sitting somewhere, you're telling him a story, you're chatting, it's great—at a bar, or the old Tavern at the Manor House, or on the bus—and some time passes and then, look! there you are in one of his books—a dubious honor at best. Now throw this into the mix: the man suffers from addiction: *alcohol, nicotine, cannabis, sex*, according to a note he has since made vanish—oh, I see it all, indeed! So many addictions, such a complicated structure of dependency—remove even the smallest part and the whole thing comes toppling down; so many addictions, and still so at odds with the world! The doctor asked him

nimble-fingered craftsman, while the dental hygienist re-marks approvingly of my stoic inertia, that it puts her in mind of a Native American. Is there any greater relief than in returning from a visit to the dentist? More than once I've left that office, leaving with it my violent agitation, left cured and thrown myself full body and spirit into the fall or spring weather, to return home in triumph. I swear by the dentist. And there's no doubt that after a single session in the dentist's chair, sitting for an hour with your jaw wrenched open, you'll leave there a better lover. — *By the way*, as the English say, was there some mention of cystic bright spots in the apices of my lungs, bullous emphysema even? How this tour guide comes by his information, now that's what alarms me. It can only have been my radiologist, Dr. Adnan El Shammah, who told him, professional confidentiality notwithstanding; there's no other way to explain it. — So I take a little peek around be-fore leaving the house? And . . . ? Did not the great tenor Fritz Wunderlich, at the height of his career, on the eve of his New York Metropolitan debut, fall and break his neck while hurry-ing carelessly down the stairs? But let's suppose I make it to my front door intact. I open the door, it creaks, I ascertain that conditions, albeit miserable and oppressive, are at least figuratively clear, so I set out, the huntsman's chorus from Weber's *The Marksman* thrumming in my head. And? What on earth can compare with the pleasure of the chase? And to leave the house and later return, having succeeded or failed but returned nonetheless, that's an accomplishment in and of itself, it's a lot less simple than it sounds, and it certainly doesn't go without saying; and then as the *shaper* of one's cir-cumstance rather than its victim, this coming and going gets even more complicated. Now then, imagine what it takes to leave the house knowing full well that every actual *victim* of circumstance appears always to his own imagination as its master, imagine what it takes leaving the house then, going on your way, the drinking song from Verdi's *Otello* upon your lips, going about your business, and after having attended to your affairs with all the attention properly due them, or if you have no affairs, then having met your obligations, or if you have none of these, simply then returning home, returning to the fold, to house and home, to wife and child, table and bed, returning to book and lamp, dog and stereo, cat and television, back to paper and pencil, bread and water . . . Where do people find the strength, I sometimes wonder, as I stand by my window or am urged along like a fish through water, bewildered, I wonder: Where do people find the strength to *go on*? How do they manage to wake up each morning and go to work? And the certainty in their steps, where do they find the self-assurance to keep on placing one foot in front of the other? But is it even personal strength that's required for any of that, isn't it rather weakness, in the end? Can it be there's some general, overriding, inscrutable force that lures, no, draws, no, better yet *sucks* the people from their homes each morning, some sort of nameless, motiveless *suck*? Could be. On the other hand, for many of them, I think, there's some actual satisfaction in taking those few steps from the house to the garage; for some of them, to be able to drive in their own cars to their offices is its own remuneration—for me this is both strange and incomprehensible. If I absolutely must leave the house, and it becomes absolutely necessary that I must deviate in either a distasteful way from the familiar path or in a familiar way from the distasteful path and strike out in some other direction, it's essential I go over it all in my mind first. So many dangers to consider! Shingles falling from roofs; buildings collapsing; tempestuous winds out of the north, vigorous gusts with speeds topping 140 kilometers an hour; out-of-control cars; run-amok citizens; recidivist criminals and first-time offenders posing a threat to my physical integrity, and spectacular suicides posing a threat to my psychic integrity—when it's no more or less than this sense of integrity, of either variety, that's enabling me to leave the

that in mind.) So be quiet, chest pain, I won't be fooled again! But this strain in my left testicle? A strain, yes, a pulling kind of pain, like the plucking of a string, like something delicately called to mind, there it is, and there again . . . ? Let there be no mistake: any sort of psychosexual origin can be ruled out right away, in my opinion. Now that I think of it, I believe it was several months ago—as far as my left testicle is concerned, though it may just as well be the right one tomorrow—that I caught a chill at the public pool, and I may have developed an infection . . . But what can you do? I'm certainly not going to show my penis, my *genitals* to my friend, the pediatrician. A urologist is out of the question, and I don't know of any women specializing in men's health. Quiet then, you stupid testicle, I've got other organs than you that are making their presence felt, my gallbladder for instance, an old acquaintance, a regular of sorts in this rather rundown establishment, she and her little children, my gallstones. It looks to me, I can already tell, that I'll have to subject her to yet another punishing cure; I'll make some devil's claw tea—since I'm not actually writing right now—a splendid medicine indigenous to German Southwest Africa, good for an all-purpose detox and beneficial for the liver, who copes, Lord knows, with her far from inconsiderable task with great steadfastness, skill, and know-how.—But that sudden sensation I had at the time, like I was walking on cotton, as though there were too little oxygen in my brain, it happened before and again after that, the *confusion*? A heart attack had been my first diagnosis, yes, my telltale heart. And I'd been ignoring, or had just gotten over, as the saying goes, a case of the flu the week before. That can't have actually been a heart attack, I thought, feverishly fixing myself something to eat, I probably just hadn't had enough breakfast. Maybe it was a silent heart attack, they say that happens, or, what's more likely in my case, an inarticulate, muttering one. No. Circulatory collapse was my next guess, but the symptoms passed, or I pulled

when accompanied by headaches, indicative of a defect in the spinal column. But I seldom have headaches, very seldom ... Agora, the marketplace, the people's assembly. Is this then my punishment for having turned my back on the masses, on the working class, without having allied myself with any other class? It's conceivable. But what do I care about the working class? I get nothing from them, no strength, no approbation; and I give them nothing, no strength, no thanks. The working class is the working class and I am myself, Jolyon Brettingham Smith, Smith, yes, like Schmidt, my name is Schmidt, I'm here for the rent—Schmidt? Oh yes, you'll be hearing from me again.—My agoraphobia is of course rooted in entirely different causes, and I'm very aware of what these are, though I'd rather not deal with them here, one needn't be so forthcoming. Besides, Weber's wild huntsmen will bring it all to a spectacular finish. And is not life, as Lampersberg writes, the sole cause of death, an extinction, a disintegration? If not organic, then psychosomatic; if not the spinal column, then the head; if not the lungs, then the liver; if not of cancer, then of the treatment; if not of the cause, then of the cure, or of a sudden case of pneumonia; if not Scylla, then Charybdis, it's all for shit, *it's all for shit*, to use the expression of a young man whose voice sometimes rises from the courtyard through the kitchen window and rings in my ears. And if you have thus far managed to avoid all of this, you'll be struck by lightning or driven into the abyss by a tour guide. So it goes.

How have I come back around to the tour guide? Yes, right, the note, where did I put it? I brought a small but very important note back from vacation with me, a little slip of paper, dear God, all these papers, here, this must be it, that's right, it says: *Köll, the architect Rogner, finish this.* Strange. But say I don't even know anyone by the name of Köll or an architect called Rogner? An industrial baker name of Schiesser I know, and a city councilman Antes, and there's a guy

I know who runs a brothel who goes by the name of—no, I've mixed things up, not Otto Waldemar Schwanz, it's Traub this time, *Lackschuh-Traub*. But an architect called Rogner ...? Don't worry, I'm only kidding. Of course I'll finish Rogner. *Literature is a fight against crime*, after all. I may very well be *at odds with the world*, but you have to finish what you've started, and this time around, there's no stopping me. Wait a minute—didn't somebody say that recently: *There's no stopping me?* That's right: a man from the southern provinces of the empire on his march to the capital, a pure-blooded politician, as they say, a self-nominated *outpost-German* whose march was financed by an inheritance acquired, let's say, by elective affinity. A born winner, they say with reverence, though the only thing he ever legitimately won was an essay-writing contest at a national youth athletic tournament, where, in ascending the podium, he cemented that boyish born-victorious pose, and there hasn't been a single crack in it since, it all froze right there, from his politics to the expression on his face, as he's tried like a man possessed to recapture, by other means, on other occasions, that long ago moment of triumph; a back-slapping, snot-nosed little brat puffing on a pipe in his lederhosen who's long overdue for a good punch in the face. Be that as it may, moving on, no Haider, no matter his first name, is going to stop me. Literature is a fight against crime, I'm drunk at the thought of it! Onward, then; onward: Who can stop a man who truly sees what he's up against? Try holding me back, you won't hold out. He who acts has understood. He who truly sees what he's up against is *insufferable*. He who has understood *this*, hesitates. Onward, onward down this street full of grievance. What a wonderful solo! The destination means nothing, the way too is meaningless. The destination is far, the way laborious. Nevertheless, onward, into the mist, toward the vague outlines that lie ahead. He who wanders has understood. Writing is mountain climbing in the mind. He who has understood and does not

What I Overheard at the Tavern at the Manor House
(*Oral History*)

It went like *this*: I was the son of a waitress, and my mother, back when the Glockner pass was being built, worked in the barracks, in the cafeteria, honest to God. And one day fire broke out in the cafeteria, and in a heartbeat everything goes up in flames, even the living quarters right next door. And in these barracks one of the engineers was keeping a very important briefcase, a briefcase full of irreplaceable things, is what he said; and here he is outside, his briefcase inside, and smoke and flames between them. So I'm—let me just say that as a boy I was above all a first-rate swimmer and diver, so, in a flash I calculate: if I can swim underwater for twenty five meters in a single breath, I think to myself, then I can easily run ten meters into the smoke and back again . . . Now I ask the engineer where exactly his briefcase is supposed to be and take a deep breath and make a break for it, and in the blink of an eye I'm back outside, briefcase in hand! And this engineer's very pleased with me, and very pleased to have his briefcase back, and he asks me what I want to be when I grow up, and I say I'd like to be a tailor . . . And I'm telling you, this engineer, I can't remember his name anymore, but out of gratitude he put me in touch with a master tailor in Salzburg, and that's how I came be a tailor's apprentice. And those Salzburg years, the privilege of learning a craft, that was only the beginning of what were to be some of the best and brightest years of my life. The master tailor was very pleased with me too and he took me to a German athletic club in Salzburg, and oh, what camaraderie I found there, between boys and girls, it was really exceptional, once in a lifetime . . . Ca-

maraderie, mind you, nothing sexual, not like nowadays . . .
This was back in the *Systemzeit*, and the master tailor, he was
in the SA, which was illegal then, and he kept weapons in
the house; later the story went they uncovered a secret ar-
senal, but that's an exaggeration, of course. So one day the
police come—they ransack the house, flash a warrant, and
take the master tailor away, just like that! But the master tailor got wind of the matter in advance and had entrusted me
with a bag, a heavy bag, and the address of a comrade in Klagenfurt, at a dance hall there, one Tanzcafé Lerch, and I was
supposed to deliver the bag to the boss. So I take the bag—
I'm sure you can imagine what was inside—I take the bag
to Klagenfurt, to this fellow Lerch. And this fellow Lerch—
I had no way of knowing at the time, I was just a kid—but
way back then he was already the boss of the illegal *Sicherhe-
itsdienst*, the SD, the secret police, and later it turns out he's
a real heavy hitter, Globe's right hand man, the right hand
man of Globocnik, and Kaltenbrunner is his man in Berlin.
This Kaltenbrunner—wait, what am I saying? I can't possibly
be drunk already! Guess that just goes to show, get a couple
of old veterans together and you never know . . . So this fellow *Lerch*, out of gratitude he refers me to a colleague of his
in Vienna, and that's how I ended up at the Quartermasters'
Academy.—*The Quartermasters' Academy!* I now heard behind me two other voices that until this point had been holding themselves back in reverent silence: The Quartermasters'
Academy, well done! Well you've sure come a long way from
G—!—The Quartermasters' Academy was only the beginning, after that I decided I'd join . . . well, I'd rather not say
aloud—continues the voice at my back; my back, though, is
broad—and in '38 things really got going . . . Later I went
off to war, and, like everyone else, just following orders, I later found myself subjected to all these crude accusations, making me out to be some sort of war criminal, you know how it
was . . . I served in Lublin and later in the Ukraine . . . Never

in Sweden, though, not like that bastard Kreisky, ha!—Oh, and how about the beard on that guy, oh that fucking beard! chimed in the two voices behind me.—Yes, yes, that swine with his fucking beard and his six million Jews! What about the three and a half million German soldiers who set out to make a better future for themselves and wound up losing their lives, what about them?—The bastard, the bastard! the other two voices spoke up in support.—Anyhow, after the collapse I left for South Africa and made a small fortune there. My eldest son lives there still, he's even been featured recently in a short write-up in the magazine *Das neue Reich*—"Das neue Reich," think about that a minute ... I've got a subscription, there's some real worthwhile reading in there, about what the future will look like, for instance: some foresee another monarchy, others a reannexation, very interesting in any case. And my other son's been over in Indonesia for a while now, he's come a long way, too; farther even than his older brother, and I bet he'll make it even farther than me, that's what I've always said.—Even so, you sure have come a long way from G—, I heard both the other voices again, all the way to South Africa and back to Munich, not bad at all!—I came to Munich to retire but I tell you I haven't had a moment's rest; if I had, I wouldn't have needed this stress cure, but the doctor says that within the month, full steam ahead, no problem. And the doctors in Munich, hats off to them, just as good now as they were back then ...—To the doctors, to the doctors! The other two cheered.—Ah, and so fate has returned me to the old stomping grounds of my youth, *that's* how it went, just like that, no two ways about it. Now, in the words of the poet, let us raise a glass, to health, to happiness, *zum Wohl!*

In the Courtyard of the Manor House
(*After Old Photos*)

In the background you can make out the fountain. In the foreground, eight members of the staff have gathered to be photographed with the adjutant to the Dutch queen, who used to summer here back in the day. Next to the adjutant—a lanky gentleman in a sporty pair of knickerbockers—sits a woman in a long pinafore stretching from her throat all the way to the ground; her hands, already showing the early signs of edema, are folded neatly in her lap. This is my great aunt, the *manor stewardess*, maiden name Benedikter. Behind her stands the chauffeur in a white uniform jacket and a cap that is balanced on a pair of broadly protruding ears. Next to him is another great aunt of mine, the *manor cook*, also born a Benedikter, though I knew her as Aunt Unterwelz, wife of the commander of the local constabulary, the retired Johann Unterwelz. My great uncle loved to hunt, loved curling and his garden, where he kept the old, traditional horticultural practices alive. He passed away the year of the revolution, 1968, at the age of forty-nine. In his garden, the estate of my childhood, not a patch of land was left uncultivated; from his herb garden I came to know fenugreek, parsley, boxwood, and marjoram. A slate that hung beside the garden gate announced in thin, cursive letters that his haunting little hybrid the *pineberry* was *for sale*; and in a region where for centuries there'd been no wine, my uncle trained his vines to grow along the southern face of the house and the two-storied woodshed, which we affectionately called the wood pile, where he pressed the grapes in a small tub in the cellar, decanted the young wine into cloudy, mismatched glass bottles, corked them, and sealed them with wax. This extraordinarily potent white wine, more of a tonic than a table wine, was a special pleasure reserved for Sunday afternoons or long winter nights, when the childless couple would sit down to a game of dominos or to "have a look" at a series of color photographs through the *viewfinder*, a stereoscopic apparatus and very rare gift in those days, given them by a relative who had emigrated overseas, my uncle in America whom I'd never met, the only son of the Benedikter family, who'd gone to the United States at the turn of the century to make his fortune and who, like the Unterwelzers, had remained childless. I, Karl Roßmann, would have been the *rightful* heir!—By now the Unterwelz home, the woodshed, and the well (my house! my wood pile! my well!) have been torn down and the garden's gone to seed, everything has been destroyed. The actual heir, a police detective and glider pilot, acting with the extreme recklessness that is so characteristic of police detectives and glider pilots both, ended up dumping all the household appliances, the garden tools, the whole interior of the house into a landfill; he razed the vegetable beds and uprooted the fruit trees (in my dreams I still roam in their shadows), had a *lawn* put in, and a modern brick shithouse—pardon me, *bungalow*—with concrete terraces built in its place. I was away in the Balkans when my great uncle died, I'd recently gotten married; of all the treasures tucked away at the Unterwelz estate, I'd only hitherto managed to salvage an herbarium dating from 1572—an authentic *Lonicerus*—as well as one demitasse and saucer. I remember my uncle's enduring question— *Why is there music?* (which was often then followed by *What is it good for?*) — to which I had still found no answer even on my last visit, not that I had any way of knowing then that it would be the last. Music of any kind was intolerable to my uncle, military marches included, which in a constabulary commander is rather surprising. So intolerable was it to him that he would curse his own frailty each summer

evening after the five o'clock news had ended and he couldn't
move his old bones quickly enough from the porch to where
the enormous radio sat inside to shut it off before the nightly
music broadcast began.

But back to the Manor House. Since the manor was situ-
ated not far from either the Benedikter hometown of Berg or
from Lienz, where the majority of my great aunts went off to
after they were married, the Benedikters and other relatives of
mine had always found work there. Not pictured in the photo, for instance, is my great uncle who died before I was born,
the *manor gardener*, who had married a Benedikter daughter
and worked for the railroad as a conductor, though his natural proclivities were fishing, botany, and astronomy. (Another
photograph, a postcard, shows him holding an immense salm-
on; on the reverse it reads, as if he'd been a man of some im-
portance—now why should I have written *as if?*— *Wilhelm
Kohler, Conductor, Lienz.* The family referred to him as simply *the botanist* or *the stargazer*: he spent his entire fortune on
stargazing and on equipment for his observatory. He built a
house in the Albin-Egger-Straße in Lienz, and over the door-
way he had the constellation Orion engraved; even though
the house, the *Villa Orion*, has since been remodeled and the
constellation as well as the trellis that used to decorate the fa-
çade have been effaced, to this day the heavy front doors still
bear the inscription: *W. K. 1908.*) —The lord of the manor,
one Baron May, a descendant of Baron May de Madiis, the
last of the guildsmen, the first to write a scholarly history of
gold mining in the High Tauern range, is not to be found
in any of the Manor House records. When the glory days of
the Manor House, as well as my aunts' terms of employment
there, came to an abrupt yet not altogether unforeseeable end,
the aged lord of the manor fled to Holland, where, the night
before his ship was to depart for asylum overseas, he shot
himself. And it was only on account of her own advanced age
that the manor stewardess, my great aunt, was spared the terror

of the Drautal SA. *Out of the way! You saw nothing!* those SA hoodlums dared shout at her as they thundered past in their trucks on their way to plunder the manor: *You saw nothing!* To think that my aunt, who was nothing if not gentle and kind, had to submit to this kind of treatment. But as it turns out, she did see a thing or two, didn't she? As a matter of fact, she saw it all, she saw everything so that one day I'd then be able write it all down—since after all my great aunt, the manor stewardess, and her great nephew, each of us has, in our own way, always been rather shrewd. I still to this very day eat off the china the lord of the manor personally bequeathed to her, long before the annexation, which she then, upon first meeting me, when I was still a toddler, had already designated as mine; and on the linens I inherited from the manor, on these cool, luxurious sheets I still sleep and partake of my carnal pleasures.

In Treuchtlingen

If only I were in Burgau, in Parschallen! Restless and help-less I wander through Treuchtlingen, I am lost, the Franco-nian mountains bear down on my brain, I'm wandering in a Franconian nightmare. I've lost my cap, and all roads lead past bratwurst stands to quarries. How can it be I've washed ashore here? Now that it's too late, now I want to remem-ber, now that I remember that it's too late. In their taverns and houses they sit at the ready, the Treuchtlingers; in the streets they lie in wait for me, because I am an outsider; I can hear them shouting from their apartments. How can these people ever have beheld the mountain gloom and mistaken it for the light of day? Night has long since fallen, the urban Nuremburg gloom could be called bright beside the night in Treuchtlingen. Oh, if only I were in Burgau, in Parschal-len! I am lost, Treuchtlingen Bluff Damnation, I think, and: Treuchtlingen Limeworks Extinction Quarry ... *Treuchtlin-gen, mein Ausreib'fetzen*, I sing out into the gloom. My head, my head! I am lost, the bratwurst must have been poisoned —
No, don't, not like that. So the bratwurst wasn't poisoned? No, under no circumstance. But what about that pretty old song, *Treuchtlingen, mein Ausreib'fetzen*? That's hardly in-spired. Limeworks Extinction Quarry? Repetition, insipidi-ty, boredom. But Treuchtlingen Bluff Damnation? Innuen-do worn thin. Nuremberg, Vienna, Villa Massimo — pitiable complaint. And Gloom Quarry Darkening, is that so bad for an *evening fantasy*? All these words belong to the estate of Kaspar of Ohlsdorf and no one else may utilize them without first having somehow made them his own. But Bernhard's narrator, wandering in the middle of the night somewhere

between Burgau and Parschallen, *found* a cap! And who's to say it wasn't *me* that lost it? Nonsense. So it's destined to remain a fragment, the start of a fragment: Restless and helpless I wander through Treuchtlingen, I am lost, the Franconian mountains—enough already, I'm not even keeping the chapter head, and for that matter, why Treuchtlingen? Well, the Treuchtlingers are the ablest painters of interiors throughout the whole of Germany . . .

I traveled to Germany to experience something. It's with this sentence, returned to my writing desk, that I'll have the chapter begin. But of course, before I can return, I'm going to have to leave. I depart in two weeks. After several postponements—Vollmer is a very busy man—the date's been set. The ticket should be waiting for me at the airport. Vollmer will be there, I was told, Vollmer will have time. Vollmer actually *has* to be there, because of the thing in Denmark, too; without Vollmer nothing will get done. As you know, my contact tells me, Vollmer's got a lot on his plate right now, he's got a sticky situation on his hands and doesn't seem to be making much headway. I was upstairs yesterday, briefly, no one heard me come in, Vollmer was sitting there in the half dark with Jacobi, imploring him, he didn't take any notice of me. And next week, as you know, next week Vollmer's getting married, so he—what? You didn't know that? I thought Vollmer would have told you, no? Oh, now I probably shouldn't have said anything, since, as you know—no, of course you don't, how on earth could you—Vollmer tends to keep his *changes of heart* to himself, or at least he doesn't bother to explain himself in the office, I just thought he would've told you about that. But of course you'd never dream of making any use of this information, of course you wouldn't, since, as you know, Vollmer is a difficult man, easily offended. But the week after next Vollmer will have time, he's—as you know, we've already had to postpone your trip once—oh, twice? Twice, yes, we've had to postpone—he's working on it, you have his word. Vollmer will be there—

And sure enough! Ten days later, the phone rings. Hold on, don't make any plans just yet, says my contact, something unexpected's come up, it's a sticky situation, Vollmer only in-

formed me of it yesterday, only yesterday I'm sorry to say—
we are of course friends, but his office is a full three doors
down from mine. In any case, a high-ranking, very important
man from Israel said he's coming—well, he told us he's coming but to be clear we invited him, like we did you, although
that was a while ago, and he only just now confirmed—he
wants to take a look around, compare this and that, and Vollmer, as you know, no, you don't know, do you? He never
told you? No. Well. Vollmer spent some time in Israel a while
back, as a guest, as part of his training, and the situation
with Israel is of course a very delicate one, so now Vollmer is
obliged to give our Israeli friend his full and undivided attention. Yes, of course he ought to have said something sooner, but you know how Vollmer is. So, hold on a while longer,
hold on until—yes, let's say mid-January, would that work
for you, mid-January? That would work great for us, Vollmer
should be back from vacation by then—he's going to Zell,
you know how he loves cross-country skiing—then you'll
have to allow him a few days to prepare, but mid-January he
should have time.

I traveled to Germany to experience something. That will
be my opening sentence, once I've returned to my writing
desk. This time it should all work out. Vollmer will be there,
he has to be, because of the thing in Denmark at least. I even
called him on his personal line and had the appointment confirmed; he'll pick me up from the airport, then we'll go to
dinner, Vollmer said so himself.—I'm traveling first to K—,
where I've got a few things to take care of, then from K— I'll
take the red-eye. But no sooner do I arrive in K— than the
inconceivable occurs: I'm notified I need to call a number in
F—, and it's urgent. So I call F— and it's my contact on the
other end of the line: I'm sorry to have to tell you this but
something rather unpleasant has happened, you know how
unpredictable Vollmer can be. In any case, he—I don't understand it myself—but he called me this morning from his

office and said in a nutshell that he'd dropped the project, the
Denmark thing too, yes, it's unbelievable, isn't it? He must
have been entertaining the thought for a while without having said anything about it, you know how Vollmer is. He's a
brilliant man, but do you think it's possible you might have
offended him somehow? He was rather brusque this morning, didn't even bother to explain; he always leaves that up
to me, which I find rather unpleasant, but what can you do?
Do you think there could be another colleague involved—
a *female* colleague, perhaps? In any case, we'll have to postpone your coming to F— indefinitely, since we'll be starting from scratch, so to speak. And your trip to B—; you
were planning to go on to B— from here, weren't you?—
yes, well you'll have to manage that on your own, at your own
expense, I mean . . . But we'll be in touch, of course, as soon
as we've found you a replacement for Vollmer, of course we
want to get you a first-rate man, and there aren't too many
of those around. This is not the first time that Vollmer's tak-
en such liberties, but the organization would rather not do
without him. One time we'd invited a guest here, a top-rank-
ing man from Israel, and Vollmer just disappeared, completely snubbed him, an Israeli no less. But we can still keep you
on, all in due time . . . In any case, be patient, you'll be hearing from us again.

in Nuremberg, the row houses there, the advertisements for *Laundromat Schmidt* pasted along the cemetery wall. I've crossed the Mill Road in Neumünster—no sniper fire, nothing. It gets better: I've been to Bielefeld, twice. The first time, however, the climate, socially speaking, prevented me from staying. Years later I tried again, successfully. I managed to spend two full nights at Hotel Bielefelder Hof, the first building on the square, just like the brochure promised, a long since abandoned, closed-down hotel right across from the train station.—But wait, closed down? How can that be, if I was staying there? I remember walking in through the revolving door, a porter in black livery suddenly appearing out of the half dark in the lobby, he wore an insignia pinned to his lapel made of two crossed, golden keys, even the elevator was working, and I was informed I'd be served breakfast in the morning ... Then again, the halls were silent and deserted, the dining room and lounge were dark, and the radiator was ice cold in the middle of winter. Still, there had to have been guests staying there other than just me, because one night after returning rather late, the porter came running and said to me, a hint of reproach in his voice: Quick, quick! Where have you been all night? Labor Minister Hierl and Defense Contractor Herr Oetker are expecting you!—No, I'm sure I must have dreamed that; there are certain German hotel rooms where I can't help but think about storm troopers passing through, it's kind of an obsession of mine: I imagine them hanging their uniforms carefully in the closet or folding them over the backs of chairs; I imagine how, in the morning, with their suspenders hanging from their waistbands, they shave and slick their wet hair back, ready for action, or how they— Enough already!—take one last look out the window before leaving the room, out over *National Uprising Square*, just like I used to look out my hotel room window onto *Resistance Square*.—Once, in Oberhausen, I was out looking for a pharmacy when I noticed two Germans in uniform ap-

water anyway, a large body of water. Later that evening, it was still light out, we went down to the shore. Storm clouds were gathering. In wicker beach chairs were sitting two women, deep in discussion—our wives. As we approached they grew silent; their expressions did not bode well. Doubtless they'd been discussing *relationship problems*, only I came out the other side just fine: the one woman couldn't and the other wouldn't dream of doing me any harm. It was the opposite for Ulrich. Just before the storm broke, we made a break for a bar called The Polar Bear. When the rain let up, we went back to the house. That night— No more, that's enough. That's enough? No more? Who calls the shots around here?!—that night there was an incident. I was sleeping with B. on a day-bed in the living room, the same room where the next day I would stumble across the diary or daybook or what have you with the last entry reading *Paul painted the window sashes*. We were smoking, while in the next room a muffled argument could be heard, we were smoking so-called Thai sticks; smoking *dope* from Thailand while vacationing by the Baltic . . . it's an experience I'll not soon forget and never capture any better than Hans Albers has already done. We smoked, then flung ourselves—wrong, first the clothing, we removed our clothing, then lay down on the bed: We indulged ourselves as we hadn't done for days. In the next room the fight between Ulrich and Eva intensified, and suddenly—here comes the incident—suddenly, when we were utterly spent and on the verge of falling asleep, suddenly the front door clicked shut, then came the sound of brisk footsteps on the gravel walk, then the garden gate whining on its hinges—Ulrich had for-saken his house and his Eva to sleep at the train station, which was even smaller than the one in Koblenz-Lützel, only slight-ly bigger than a beach chair. The forsaken woman was in no way distraught or even unhappy about his departure, on the contrary. Ah, how a woman can ruin a man—effortlessly. About an hour later the garden gate went—that is, the garden gate did not *go*, a garden gate cannot do that, rather *someone* went through the garden gate, as footsteps on the gravel walk testified, and again the front door clicked shut; there followed a racket in the foyer — Ulrich pulling down the extension ladder as he proceeded to set up camp for the night in the attic, amid all the junk, his very own *Night Camp in Granada* ... I can scarcely conceive what might have happened had we — in the course of my field research in Germany I was always coming across people who swore the stuff sent them into a real frenzy — had we made it a threesome and been caught in the act by the man of the house upon his return! What an experience that would have been, what a story, presuming I'd have come out the other side of *that* able to tell it — a narrow escape from *hell on the dock* at Sierksdorf ... But then I might never have discovered that lovely little commonplace book that had been hidden away: *Paul painted the window sashes* ... — So now you see: name me a place, and I've been there. Onto Buchschlag, then — yes, I've even been to Buchschlag. Ah, Buchschlag, what a story that was, with Ruth, or Edith ... No, it wasn't Ruth, or Edith. Renate, her name was Renate. Ruth, or Edith, that's another story, more recent ... or is it rather an age-old story? At the moment I don't think I could say for sure whether the story even happened to me ... Me, who? I, Jolyon Brettingham Smith? Is one I not as good as the next? I, Chinese Fritz, or I, Mister Joe? I, Wilfrid Schulz, and Renate (not my Renate but another of whom someone else says *my Renate*, the Wilfrid-Schulz-Renate, *Farewell, Mister Joe, your friends Wilfrid Schulz and Renate*, this Renate) ... Where was I? — Yes, Buchschlag, that's where, I'm sure. Do you think that our feelings, she said, Renate did (mind you: not the Wilfrid-Schulz-Renate), do you think that our feelings for each other will last even if we don't see each other again for six months? A couple of lovely nights in a little hotel room by the sea, it may turn out to have been only that, I answered. (Feelings, always these

one of my sense organs that seemed to me entirely super-
fluous in this dining car was my nose. Stuffed pig stomach
with sauerkraut, bockwurst with potato salad, cabbage with
smoked sausage, crap with sauce, how it all came reeking out
of that kitchen! So I was forced to resort to a liquid lunch,
J&B Rare Whiskey and a pilsner, which, Lord knows, I didn't
find too terrible a compromise.—Calm and comfortable,
the situation perfectly under control, I stretched my legs out
under the table and began to rummage around in the general hum, to poke around in the scraps of conversation, to
sound out if there might be anything suitable here for me.—
Be that as it may, everyone knows them as the Dalton Gang,
no one knows why, but the instant the two of them show
up, everyone cheers the Daltons are here! Hmm, could that
be a *bit* sarcastic—? Yeah well, I don't know, the Daltons,
maybe not.—I'm a doctor, I live across the street, I heard
gunshots, I tell them, I heard them, the gunshots—another male voice, to a female counterpart—But do you mean to
say they'd—? No, nothing of the sort, this world is an abyss,
an abyss . . . No, that's no good. And what did the man look
like? What—? What the man *looked like*? No one asked that,
I'm an ear witness—oh, I get it, I, as the *narrator*, am being
asked what the doctor looked like. Please, don't ask—or do,
go right on ahead and ask, but I will not describe him. One
thing's for sure: He was not wearing a maroon-colored sweater-vest, now please don't interrupt me again or I'll leave out all
the best parts. (If you find this all too confusing, no one's pre-
venting you from shutting the book or doing with it as you
see fit. Fine, now you're furrowing your brow, but have you
considered it's not just reading but writing too that's an anar-
chic act? Not that I'm not fully in command when it comes
to tense sequencing, but if I, as I traveled through Germany, without warning choose to express myself in the present
tense, it will be, should you choose to read on, understood
as the voices in my mind.) To return then: I poked around

in the scraps of conversation without yet having found anything suitable for use.—I'm not under any illusions here: If
this publisher refuses to keep my books in print—I've been
put off one too many times, and this putting-off is not only
off-putting but it's really starting to put me out when I think
of all the off-putting crap he puts out for—so if he refuses to keep them in print, I'm done for, *and* I'm done with
the entire business, though it's true I would've written them
regardless . . . I heard a voice behind me, an extremely em-
bittered voice speaking behind my head; the man must have
been, like me, leaning very far back in his chair.—Imagine it:
a living author whose books are out of print, it's maddening,
it's grotesque! Sure, when an author's dead and buried, maybe then his books will be revived, but even that's far from certain.—This sounded interesting, promising even, this should
suit me fine in fact. I'll listen in for a while. Until the ticket
collector makes an appearance, I'll pursue these voices behind
my head; or should I say, allow them to pursue me?—Now,
if I were Italian or even just wrote in Italian, that would help,
since this guy not only publishes translations from Italian but
he'll do anything for the Italians, there's no trade deficit too
great for him. What can you do, he *loves* Italian literature, he
finds it so *demented*, and funny! He loves Italian literature the
way the English love *the arts*—if you've ever heard an Eng-
lishman say *Oh, I love the arts*, then you know what I mean.
He loves Italian literature so much that everyone at the office
has taken to saying *scusi* when they get in each other's way.
Is that ridiculous or what? And do you know what this publisher has taken the liberty of doing? He's written me a letter in which he implies I've duped *him*, cheated *him*, plain
and simple! Here—it sounded as though he was pulling a
sheet of paper from his bag, and the speed with which he did
so suggested to me that he'd often reached for this sheet of
paper to annoy any number of others with its contents, but
this only fascinated me all the more.—Here: After my first

book, which was *excellent*, as he so generously concedes, I basically handed over nothing but trash for the second, *the two texts are essentially incommensurate*, as he puts it, look, it's all right here. And he writes this *after* the book's already come out, it's obscene, isn't it? No one treats me this way and gets away with it! An appropriate response will occur to me soon enough, I'm still thinking it over. A publisher does indeed have it in his power to ruin an author; though on the other hand, when faced with an author's vengeance, he's powerless to defend himself. — Or take for instance the poster scenario: When we print a *new book*, we design a *new poster*, he promised me years ago, realizing, as you do, that women have been known to hang these posters up in their rooms; a poet ought not merely write well, he ought to look good, too, isn't that right? But moving along: the book had only just come out, I'd hardly begun to press him about the poster, when he told me straight to my face that he had no intention of keeping his promise, a poster costs an arm and a leg and the booksellers only throw them out anyway. But of course he has posters made for all the new Italian releases! And the very same bookstores that in my case would only have *thrown them out anyway*, these he inundates with posters of the Italians — when what I'm told is that *phone calls or postcards will do*! It's unbelievable all that this man has squeezed from me already, absolutely unbelievable! And Lord knows how god-awful these other guys' posters are . . .

I've heard enough. It's time to bring out the ticket collector. Across from me, three young women — two with their backs to me — sat down and ordered wine. At the exact instant I decided it was time for him to appear, the ticket collector was already approaching from the narrow aisle next to the kitchen and asking these women to produce their tickets; then he made his way slowly through the car and — am I hearing this right? — said without thinking to each table as he passed, first left, then right, enjoy your meal, *bon appétit . . .!*

I ought to tell you, though, while we're at it, that I'm not by nature a whiskey drinker; in fact, I prefer vodka, though only the finest, of course, and that's why, in this dining car, I've had to switch to vodka—wait. What am I writing? Is it the alcohol?—I've had to switch *to whiskey*, there we go.) I readjusted myself in my seat and decided to rummage around again in the general hum, specifically in the scraps of conversation I could catch from the three women sitting across from me. (In Amsterdam, at the flea market, aptly termed— it's true, my travels to Germany often lead me far beyond the German border—in the flea market in Amsterdam on a chilly November day, I stood watching a man, a gaunt man in a long shabby coat, as he bent over and dug through a pile of clothes on the pavement. Engrossed and unwavering, he groped about in this junk heap of clothes for worn and discarded women's underwear. Each pair he found he held up, scrutinizingly, against his nostrils. He then either pocketed them or reluctantly let them fall. His nose had grown red and inflamed from all his prodding around in search of whatever secret messages these panties may have held for him, from poking around in those dead letter boxes. What would you call the perversion that overpowers a pitiable creature such as this? Fetishism it's not, but some kind of syndrome, *Süskind Syndrome*, can that be it? As ever.)—No to Kreiensen, darling, I'll be no one's maternity temp, I heard one of the three women saying.—And what does that piece of shit say to me? I'm retiring soon, allow me just this ...! So I go to Junior— no sense in taking it to the old man, he'll just sit there drooling over your tits, Old Schmidt—so I go to Junior and make it very clear: Not me and no to Kreiensen. (Well? I don't know ... No, not *well, I don't know*, I'll cross that out, there.) Where was I? Oh yes: not me, and no to Kreiensen.—Oh, I was so relieved, said the woman who sat with her face— among her other lovely attributes—angled in my direction, *I was so relieved when I got pregnant and could finally drop out of university* . . . Ah, what a statement, what a find, that really got my blood pumping! Now I was convinced this train had penetrated *deep* into Germany. Yes, well, how to describe her, this woman, when, in view of any woman, my mind goes straight to the gutter? Be quiet! The third woman spoke in a low voice as she leaned in over the table. —Let's talk this out, I say to him: what does it actually mean to you, to sleep with me? And do you know what that pig replied? Fucking, it's just a break between cigarettes. Who ever heard of such a thing?! So of course I tell him, well if that's the case, it's best that you leave, get out of here right now, you're one fucked up guy . . . I'll tell you what a relief it was to be able to terminate that pregnancy . . . The three women sat huddled close together. — Same here, I heard the first one again, the not-me and no-to-Kreiensen voice. He could at the very least have made me come once in a while, you know? He thought having sex in the shower was stupid . . . And when he was full, that was especially disgusting . . . He had this white silk scarf he'd be wearing when he'd come sailing through the door, always with the same old song, *Ist denn kein Stuhl da, Stuhl da, für meine Hulda, Hulda* . . . One time, it was a horrible night, the worst night, I screamed at him, Paulus, right now, you couldn't even get it up if you tried . . . And he takes another swig and goes: Yeah? Well, so what? I'm not even trying . . . So, yes, I was relieved when I got pregnant and could liquidate *that* useless partnership . . .! (*Liquidate* . . . interesting choice of words. I think I'd only ever heard, well, apart from the meaning the word acquired in recent German history— yes indeed, and should they, the Germans that is, care to emerge from the shadow of the Third Reich, by all means: but let it be *with hands raised,* with *both* hands raised, mind you, or better yet, clasped behind their heads—I think I'd only ever heard that word used before about an ice hockey match, some player had chased the puck all the way into the goal, *liquidating* the goalie, and scoring a point. But see, there you go: I travel to Germany to experience something and I learn something new in the process.)

Thanks to that train of thought, I've missed out on the women's apparently sudden departure—or did I nod off for a minute? Only wine bottles and glasses remain on the table across the aisle. Which reminds me, have I already ordered another whiskey, and what about the pilsner? Oh, it's all right here. These blackouts, these spells of amnesia, I don't know, was it—was it—what's the reason they keep giving me? Now I forget. I looked out the window; a station called Eschwege came briefly into view and receded. I moved my legs a little under the table—eleven hours in the dining car, an extreme athletic challenge, it demands a great deal of physical control. I stretched out my legs again and leaned back, back into the broadcast range of the voices behind my head.—January 28, 1986: Were you watching the news that night? When the space shuttle exploded? Ah, what a pleasant evening that was, and what incredible color! Like an Antonioni, only better! I can't remember the last time the news put me in such a cheerful mood, certainly not since Hinckley made an attempt on the life of that son of a bitch, that plague of a US president— ah, but all the more disappointing that he didn't succeed. The evening of January 28, though—pure pleasure, and danger- ous too! Just imagine if the shuttle had exploded out in space . . . So very dangerous! Which raises a basic question: whether humanity will survive the Americans, or the Americans sur- vive humanity. Why doesn't this nation of criminals just take off, the whole lot of them, for some other planet and leave the rest of us in peace? As you can see, I make a clear distinc- tion between humanity and Americans, though one ought to concede the Americans the possibility of becoming human, more than that, force them to it . . . But what force on earth is in a position to do that? Misery, misery, everywhere you look . . . this miserable reality, miserable literature, all this repetiti- veness—miserable . . . The misery of literature, indeed! Why is it that some people write so much, can you answer me that? Some people can't let a year go by without writing a new play, a new book, and all they're doing is repeating themselves ... Not a year goes by without the media igniting and ruthlessly fanning the flames of some new scandal. Take what happened to B., for instance! ... Death, desolation, grotesqueries—call them gargoyles if you like. ... gloom, malice ... The voice, softer now, began spluttering these words like curses, causing me to pay closer attention still. Malice, gloom, *possession* ... All of it, malicious ... I'm sure that right now he's sitting at his desk, in the gloom, in his old farmhouse gloom, which for him is the gloom of the world itself, writing ... Writing himself deeper into world literature, so they claim, hoarding the finest stockpile of obsessions in all of Upper Austria ... While I travel, he sits in his clinic, his private madhouse, and writes ... He's writing himself an edge, he's writing himself further into the lead ... I travel, he writes, I can hardly believe it ... It's true, the more you're written about, the more you write ... Malicious is what it is ... Let him sit there, then, in the gloom of his rustic clinic, let him sit there in his farmhouse, in his Black Forest clinic, and write ... in the gloom of his Black Forest clinic, he and his lung condition, just let him! We'll see soon enough who the master of the grotesque is, who's the *real country doctor*!—Or take this other idiot with his own nervous affliction, his water retention, sitting there eclipsed beneath his waterfall gloom at Bad Gastein, let it be an agony for him to retain water or to pass it ... Another B., this one a Burger, with cheese ... Swiss, too ... Mr. Swiss Cheese, come in please ... What an unpalatable idiot and pedantic philistine, and he can have that in writing, he can go ahead and sue me ... But nobody sues me, who would do me the courtesy? For years now I've been working on it, with increasing flagrancy, and to no avail ... Crime has a name and an address—I believe this, and have always acted accordingly—and still: nothing. Nobody's calling the authorities on me, quite intentionally of course ... Not that I'm eager to give an account of myself—I can't even imagine what that would be like, standing before a tribunal—then again, the free publicity, the feedback, that's what they begrudge me! It's a conspiracy, but it's more than that: it's more like a book burning, only all the pages are blank in the first place ... There's a lot of talk about the *explosive power* of literature— yeah, right. I can write what and how I want, I can indict, on paper, whomsoever I please, and it'll get overlooked; overlooked, yes, that's a good way of putting it. What could be worse for a *publication* than being *overlooked*? Doubtless they have it out for me, only they're biding their time until I choke on my own impotence. For years now there's been a conspiracy against me, it's been objectively verified, a conspiracy of the so-called literary public—no, it's bigger than that: it's a worldwide conspiracy, a worldwide literary ... no, a *Weltliteratur* conspiracy! My books don't get translated. I've hardly had a letter in years. Whenever the phone rings, it's only because there's been a misunderstanding, or it's regarding some triviality, or the line simply goes dead. I don't get any more announcements about literary prizes; isn't that strange? No. It's not strange at all. It only goes to show exactly how tight my theory is, how deep this thing runs. Sometimes, for hours on end, I'll rehearse the scene—pacing back and forth between the kitchen and the hall, my end of the conversation lacking for nothing in vehemence or clarity—*in my mind,* mind you; I don't move my lips when speaking with people who aren't there, I'm not crazy, after all. An objectively verified conspiracy, as I've already mentioned. As if that weren't already enough: the world literature conspiracy will not stop making fun of me! Get this: I'm sitting in the Park Hotel, it's midmorning, almost noon, I'm drinking coffee and waiting for a phone call. At some point my name actually is called, so I get up to walk over to the phone booth, when, directly in front of me, though seated a bit nearer to the phone than I, a smartly dressed young man I hadn't noticed before stands up and casually proceeds to the phone booth, as though he happens to answer to the same name and was likewise expecting a call. I follow him and listen as he answers the phone: *Kofler here.* How far will his audacity drive him, I wonder, as I stand poised expectantly nearby . . . But, as quickly becomes clear from the details of his conversation, the phone call wasn't for me after all, my suspicion dissolves, and I retreat, and this man too—need I add that he's wearing a maroon-colored sweater-vest?—returns to his table after hanging up. As far as I'm concerned, I'm the only one that goes by my name, and yet there are indeed others, I think, bewildered. I've only just noticed the two girls sitting at the man's table; they're middle schoolers as far as I can tell from their conversation—I told you I hear everything—and the man would appear to be a middle school teacher. Then he begins to pull books out of his bag, which he proudly assures the girls he bought a long time ago. None of mine are among them, I ascertain at a glance—I told you I see everything. This man is also a book-overlooker, he even overlooks books published under his own name, I go on thinking; and now this idiot is taking out a so-called best-seller list he's torn from some German news magazine (a *news* magazine, aha! I think, a *bulletin*) and he grabs a pen and begins, while loudly blathering on, to check off all the titles he already has on his shelf at home—there's only two that he hasn't got yet, though some of the others he's read twice to make up for it. Before my very eyes, and under my own name, no less, this man offers a panegyric to the institution of the best-seller list, going on about how they keep you so wonderfully up-to-date—this can't be an accident, this man knows exactly what he's doing, he's making fun of my literary misfortune in addition to making fun of literature itself. He's a collaborator in the world literature conspiracy! So what do you suppose I do? I leap to my feet, storm over to this unworthy doppelgänger's table and say: Moron! Idiot!

But he just smirks and holds up a book, *Perfume: The Story of a Murderer*, and replies: Literature, *great* literature . . . Aha! — I think — I knew it! And I bet that phone call was for me after all. So I grab the guy by his maroon-colored sweater-vest and yank him out of his chair, but before I can do any real damage, the waiter hurries over and intercedes. Of course I'm immediately thrown out of the place. — Misery, misery . . . Miserable reality, miserable literature . . .

The voice fell silent. And fall silent it must. For otherwise how could I have heard the next voice, that of our interdisciplinary ticket collector, who, as you're about to read, will now try his hand at the art of rhyme. Ladies and Gentlemen, came the ticket collector's voice over the intercom, *Coffee, tea, snack buffet — in our dining car, we do it your way!* Today's special recommendation: our homemade cheesecake . . . Germany Coffee Hour, Germany Railway, I thought, stretching out my legs under the table, Germany Cabbage, Germany Cheesecake . . . How tired I felt all of a sudden, how bored, how absolutely beat! And I didn't even have my Beckett with me; had I brought my beloved Beckett along, I might have been able to take it out and read some of my beloved Beckett, but I had left the book at home. *At home*, that's nice, I thought, *at home*, and where would that be? Under the roof over my head, under the attic over the automobile trafficker in the apartment below mine, would that be at home? At home in the sinking terrain, on the sagging floorboards, through which, day in and day out, I'm assaulted by the sound of violent disputes that will not cease until — when, already? oh sweet silence! — one of the two of them finally manages to silence the other for good?! There, where my writing desk stands, is that where I'm at home? At home among secondhand bookshelves and hand-me-down furniture, at home on chairs stolen from the waiting rooms of abandoned dentist's offices? In a bathtub in the kitchen? Beside a stove in the bathroom? Would either of these be *at home*? There, where my writing desk stands,

voice behind me. But you know what? F— writing books, F— it! From here on out, I'm writing exclusively for the *stage*, for the *spoken word*, I have drafts already at hand, drafts and notes! I've even got two pieces—dialogues, two theater-annihilating dialogues—down on paper, though I haven't brought either one to the stage, properly speaking. The first theater-annihilating dialogue, a teaching play à la Brecht, I gave up on, given that the means weren't terribly forthcoming about what the end was to be. I shelved that one around the same time I shelved my *Look of Terror*. In this piece I intended to pose and then consider the question, *McDonald's: wherefore and what for?* but the thing wasn't quite up to snuff, which I had a hard time admitting to myself. You see, if one actually means to answer the question "McDonald's: wherefore and what for?" one only finds oneself confronted with more questions still: *Union Carbide: wherefore and what for?* or *Dow Chemical* or *Coca-Cola*, wherefore and what for, the Mafia and Cosa Nostra, because the question that follows on "McDonald's: wherefore and what for?" is in fact the question of *organized crime*, and the whole of economic life in the United States is nothing if not a question of organized crime. Wherefore and what for, this American president, who doesn't *have* but *is* a cancer, that is the question! But like I said, this piece failed on the page, save for the line *Come unto me, Weinberger, in that magnificent maroon-colored sweater-vest of yours*—it's a great line, isn't it? Other than that, I have to say the whole thing was a failure. But what about the other piece, you ask. My second attempt to destroy the theater was also foiled, this time though by the performance itself, which, by the way, took place in one of those basement theaters . . . Instead of the theater, or rather instead of *theatricality itself* being exploded onstage, the staging—in express contravention of my wishes, not to mention my stage directions—*restored* the theater; theatricality was salvaged rather than laid waste to—I'm telling you: the pure animosity, the sheer stupidity! Rather than

got at the end of his name, even less what his first name is (which reminds me, I was also in the Klagenfurt New Year's Eve performance of *Die Fledermaus*)—no Strauß was ever a worth a dime as a composer, but that one, the Strauss with the double *S*, with the SS on the end of his name—clever, no?—he's the most repugnant of them all. And though I can say I feel completely at home with *The Magic Flute* and *Otello*, I haven't ever seen *The Magic Flute* or *Otello* performed in any other opera house, not even for the sake of comparing how the other extras portray their Moorish slaves or raise their trombones; how the other officers of the watch post themselves to the battlements or other minstrels prance around the table in *The Marksman*—I've never even thought to compare. But for my own City Theater piece, my own dialogue with musical accompaniment, I will bring my experience, my Klagenfurt Theater praxis to bear; my early work in the Klagenfurt Theater will come in very handy for what I have in mind. I'm really going to let the theater have it, *and how!* This is what I like to tell myself. The theater burning to the ground as the world goes up in flames, I've written it all down somewhere, the world burning to the ground as the theater goes up in flames. The production as theater, the direction as performance, the rehearsals as dialogue, all accompanied by music from *The Magic Flute!* What seems at first like the scene proper will turn out to be the rehearsal, what looks like the chaos and madness of rehearsal will be the actual piece itself, it's quite a production I've got in mind! All the same, it's not that I've got anything against the City Theater itself, on the contrary. I love the City Theater, even *The Magic Flute* they put on back in the 1964–65 season was quite the production, a remarkable cast, a seamless performance. Picture it: the man who played Papageno went on from Klagenfurt to make a name for himself internationally; the erstwhile Klagenfurt City Theater Papageno now sings at the Vienna State Opera as well as in Salzburg, and you can hear him as Papageno on the recording they made under Karajan's direction. Pamina came to Klagenfurt from a music academy in Greece and went on from there to the Munich State Theater at Gärtnerplatz. Papagena, one of Klagenfurt's most solid local talents, went on to sing at Innsbruck; the Queen of the Night came from Graz and returned to the Graz Opera; Sarastro was played by a junior high school principal from St. Viet an der Glan; the First Priest who was brought in from Romania has since become the Vienna State Opera's first ever talent agent. And lastly, Tamino was played by a young Swede who, after the show closed, slipped out of view. The two armored men — *he who wanders this street full of grievance*, you're familiar with this enigmatic chorus, aren't you?— in any case, the two armored men, one from Serbia and the other Bavaria, stayed on in Klagenfurt at the City Theater, and within fifteen years both were dead; and Monostatos, who came from Bohemia and who was also my Moorish slave driver on the stage, he stayed on in Klagenfurt, too, and likewise died. I like to joke that I'm the only one that neither stuck around Klagenfurt till the final curtain call nor managed to make a go of it anywhere else — the conspiracy, as you know. Even the guest appearances back then made their impression on me! There I stood on stage alongside the great *Kämmersänger* Rudolf Christ, alongside William Blankenship who came all the way to Klagenfurt from Texas, alongside the hoary Helge Rosvaenge and the magnificent Anton Dermota — they all gave guest performances as Tamino: Ms. Rosvaenge, who had to have been over seventy at the time, sang Tamino, and Anton Dermota sang Tamino, the same Dermota who nine years before not only brought Florestan new life but also helped resurrect the Vienna State Opera itself at the grand reopening performance of *Fidelio* — in fact he sang the part so enchantingly that even the music correspondent for the *Times* of London, the fearsome Reger, had to applaud him. So you see, my dear Atzbacher: Klagenfurt brought everyone together, under the direction of Otto Hans Böhm,

doned industrial quarter, near the frozen harbor, in front of the pointlessly renovated old post office, *Zeitkultur am Hafen* ... I retrieved my bag and hobbled on. No, it wasn't the alcohol that caused me to fall like that, nor was it the tour guide's curse, call himself what he will, neither Köll's nor Reiser's revenge—I wouldn't fall for something like that—it wasn't his or their fault I fell on my head, out of which Köll and Reiser had been sprung in the first place, and anyway my right hand, my guiding hand, the dread right hand, ever at the service of the left, this hand had been spared. No, *relief* was the reason I hadn't been paying attention, relief that soon I'd be leaving the old post office behind, relief at leaving Linz altogether, it was relief that caused me to turn my head as I walked, for one last look and to bid these cold accommodations good-bye and good riddance.—And now it seems I'll have to go back there after all, if only to set fire to the old post office since, on the train, on the return trip to my writing desk, my arm had already started aching and I was unable to straighten it, or bend it, or turn it; with the aid of my right hand I had to keep repositioning and supporting it to keep the pain at bay. This injury brought back memories ... Back then, this was a long time ago, it was my right elbow I'd hurt, the radial head, the *caput radii*, to be exact; and it wasn't any sense of relief but a very particular kind of stress that was to blame—my long-term girlfriend was about to walk out on me—and that injury had put me in a cast for two months. Now though it seemed to be the left radial head or the radius itself that had been injured. Already that evening, every movement of my uninjured right arm—even the most basic movement, say bringing a glass to my lips—triggered a reflex in my left arm, a kind of spasm that went arm in arm with a sharp pain—arm in arm? oh dear; it's a challenge, describing pain, nearly impossible, as is the description of its twin, lust; yes, lust, how to describe that ... *I was so aroused it defies description*, that's right, isn't it? How does one describe it,

And Vollmer—we've already gone over that too? That too. Yes, well, I don't know, is it the alcohol, that's missing I mean? I'll order another whiskey, that should fortify me enough to make it through this experience. There it is! Hear that? It doesn't stop, *it does not stop*, this voice!—My dialogue set to music—do you hear that?—won't have recourse to *The Magic Flute* the City Theater put on back in '64–65, but—just listen now, listen—further back, on *The Magic Flute* put on in 1942–43 by a little so-called Outpost Theater company. I'm going to do a National Socialist treatment of *The Magic Flute*, a *Magic Flute of the Stone Age*, a *German Federal Bureau of the Musical Arts and Armed Forces Magic Flute*! Oh yes: I'll take on the relationship between art and reality, taking *The Magic Flute* from the winter of 1942–43 as my inspiration: I'll stage my own *Nazi People's Welfare and District Propaganda Magic Flute*, my own *Winter Relief and Nazi Soup Kitchen Magic Flute*, my *Magic Flute of the Stone Age*! District SS commanders in attendance at a performance of *The Magic Flute*— incredible to think about, isn't it? But it happened ... What else in *The Magic Flute* was lost on a National Socialist, I'll ask, if not this saturation of art with life? Inside: *The Magic Flute*, outside: National Socialism! Inside: the coloratura of the Queen of the Night, the art, the final apotheosis, *the entire theater transformed into a sun*, and outside: reality, reality transforming itself into a hyper-organized Stone Age, into a firestorm! A theatrical sun and the world in flames, that's the treatment. *Bringing to light*, as the Philosopher B. writes, that which *ought not* remain in shadow, as I say, brought to light in the Stone Age, brought to light by fire each time ... All reality proceeds with the *not-yet* latent within it, writes this philosopher with respect to *The Magic Flute* (he has a very high opinion of Sarastro, by the way. I don't; the name itself has such a gloomy ring to it), though I would add: every not-yet may well progress to a *not-ever*. But is that reason enough to acquiesce to this so-called reality, to any old reality at all?

That's what I'll be exploring in my dialogue set to music, in my City Theater piece. I see hovering before my eyes a treatise on the theater industry's lack of character and *The Magic Flute's* indelibility—or will it rather be a treatise on *The Magic Flute's* lack of character and the indelibility of the theater industry? Was *The Magic Flute* somehow profaned by the performances in those days, that is the question: Did art, in its performance, stand in opposition to reality, or did reality, in its performance, goose-step all over art? It's unthinkable, really: on stage at the Outpost Theater: resplendence, *Elysium*, triumphal chords, the land of triumph, according to Philosopher B., Pamina's image as erotic promise—and all around, the National Socialist Stone Age reality! Art surrounded, art held hostage to reality. Did art resist reality, or reality art, that is the question. There's nothing to be gained from an art in the service of reality, any more than there is to be had from a reality that's conducive to art. *Art must destroy reality*, and have done with it, destroy reality rather than submit to it, and this applies to writing as well ... But the appalling thing, you should know, the appalling thing is: Reality carries unabashedly on, reality does not give a shit about the damage inflicted upon it by art, reality is shameless, shameless and incorrigible ... It is the unregenerate despot whichever path it takes, be it capitalist or National Socialist or revisionist ... No reality-destroyer knows this better than I do ... Time and again, I say: *Come unto me, reality*, let's settle the score, I mistreat it too, *and how*—and still: It carries all the more impudently on ... To be sure, it's better to be right and run counter to the masses than to err alongside them, but a reality-destroyer like me remains sitting powerless at his writing desk, at the mercy of the news that beleaguers him, hobbling after events that exhaust him ... Reality retaliates, formidably so. And this is exactly the reason I'm going to throw the theater at least, the theater-reality, right off stage, right into the deep end of the orchestra pit ... *City Theater*, a dia-

logue set to music ... *The Outpost Theater Magic Flute* ... Ha!
... And how, you ask, have I come by my particular knowledge about the Stone Age Magic Flute from the '42–43 season? Well, I just so happen to be in possession of a number of issues of the *National Socialist Women's League* magazine, the *Ostmark Weekly*, and — maybe I've mentioned this already? — my wonderfully informative *Faithful Eckart*. Faithful Eckart's "Carinthian Culture Report," which was published, by the way, by Bruno Brehm, is where I find all I could ever wish to know — and then some — about *The Magic Flute* from the winter of '42–43 ... All I have to do is open up my *Faithful Eckart* to experience the *glittering premier* in early December, the cheerful evenings amid such trying times; and as for Hanns Gobsch's *Mary Queen of Scots: A Drama of Passion* that ran shortly thereafter — to the warmest applause — and as for the world premier of Sittenberger's *Storm Over the Land: Scenes from the Heroic Struggle of Carinthia* — which was given a most enthusiastic reception — I can rely on *Faithful Eckart* to report all this to me. I open up my *Faithful Eckart* and can't, for all my astonishment and the grimness of my laughter, tear myself away. I open up *Faithful Eckart* and stumble upon the names of old acquaintances, names I know from my schooldays, teachers and poets personally and painfully familiar to me; Carinthia is that classical country of the didactic poet, the pedagogue who takes up the pen ... It's absolutely unbelievable the kind of creatures that were bringing young men up to be teachers back in the era of the Outpost Theater and the wartime *Magic Flute*, even in the era of the City Theater *Magic Flute*. I open up my *Faithful Eckart* and read work from the pens of my former professors, from the pens of these Ostmark and Südmark poets, about the Carinthians' *longing for empire, for a leader* ... And it was from ex-criminals like these that I had to suffer abuse as a student, just imagine ... But, like I've said, for what I've got in store, *Faithful Eckart* is absolutely priceless, he truly is a faithful Eckart, an Eckart

who won't let you down, this *Faithful Eckart* that I fundamentally and deeply detest is worth more to me than any beloved Pascal, any beloved Montaigne, any beloved Beckett . . . They must have been wonderful, I often imagine them, evenings in the Advent season, the Klagenfurters' longing for a leader sated, wartime winter again blanketing the countryside, the district propaganda minister's enthusiastic applause; I imagine dropping by Café Lerch after the performance, a highly esteemed and prosperous establishment, then as well as now; I imagine the proprietor Lerch has just come home on leave and is entertaining his guests with stories of his work in Lublin and of his immediate superior Globotschnigg, good ole Globe . . . It's curious, really, all the things that can be made to coalesce around *The Magic Flute* . . . Now then, my dialogue set to music obviously won't be *realistic* drama in any sense, it's meant to be a stunt, really. Here's how it'll work: I'll displace parts of the music from the libretto, *free them from the plot*, so to speak . . . Just imagine: the stage is dark and empty, all you hear is an aria sung by the Queen of the Night, it's genius . . . Or how about my final apotheosis: the empty stage bathed in radiance, and from *off off stage*, as we in the business say, the finale sounds, "Heil sei Euch Geweihten" . . . and all of a sudden there's a total power outage — planned, of course, but who's going to know that? — no light, no sound, *darkness and silence*, that is to say terror, it will end in terror, is that not a brilliant theater-destroying idea? Of course there will be traces of plot, fragments, a dictator-director, Sarastro's reflection, as I've already mentioned, will take the stage and direct *The Magic Flute*. In the course of rehearsal the actors will strike and refuse to obey the dictator-director . . . At some point slogans will be scrawled all over the set, all over the backdrop of the temple, the walls and columns of the shrine will be graffitied and profaned . . . *Sarastro Assassin* and *SA SS Sarastro*, the slogans will read, *Sarastro and his Apollonian Stag Party*, and *Sarastro the Light of the Aryan*

Race, or even: *Down with the Sun Temple, Clear the Stammtisch!* The dictator-director will have to act like he's having a fit, of course, when he reads that—he'll fly into a rage. Sarastro, the name itself already sounds so dungeon-masterly ... Unlike Philosopher B., I could never see what was so attractive in this character anyway; I've always been more drawn to the Queen of the Night, the cold beauty of her coloratura, absolutely first rate ... This Sarastro is in essence a ruthless god, and even amid the radiance of his sun temple, Sarastro will always remain for me the shady character that he is ... that he is ... that he is ...

The voice behind my head grew fainter and fainter and suddenly was gone; one minute there, the next minute gone! Oh sweet silence, sweet relief! Now I'm free to rummage again among these scraps of conversation to my heart's content.—I was so relieved, I heard one woman say to two others, so relieved when I had an orgasm at last and could be done with Professor Bornemann once and for all ...—We were never able to have sex, the second was saying, without taking all these precautions, on vacation, in hotels, and the amount of it, God that was awkward for me ... for years I wondered if squirting like that was normal and what kind of fluid that even was ... And then, oh, I was so relieved when I learned what the G-spot was, the *Gräfenberg zone*, and that it was related to that, then I was actually kind of proud ... Dr. Stifter even ordered a lab test done on me, for his research project!—For me, though, the third voice spoke in a near-whisper, for me it was such a relief just to have him *in there*, I completely let go, and screamed and bit and scratched ... Oh, was I ever relieved when Michael closed the door behind him and took me in his arms ... Oh, what a relief it was when Blake finally came back and I was able to confide everything ... Oh, it was such a relief when I met Adam—finally I had someone to think about while masturbating.

Oh, was I ever relieved when the train finally stopped so I

could get a break from this trip; what a relief it was to stand up from my writing desk, push in my chair, and put out the light.

It's midnight. Rain beats against the windows. I'm sitting at my writing desk. The treatment sits in front of me. I'm writing. I write: I'm at the scene of the crime. I write: One day a television producer approached the author Schmidt with an invitation to write a teleplay for the TV series *Scene of the Crime*, keeping in mind that the actors Jaggberg, Janisch, and Herz-Kestranek would be cast as detectives Hirth, Fichtl, and Schulz. Schmidt accepted the invitation, proceeded forthwith to his desk, and began to sketch out the treatment. I write: Thus Schmidt wrote: Scene of the Crime. *My name is Schmidt.* Content: The author S. is invited to write a teleplay for the TV series *Scene of the Crime*. On the producer's order, the script will feature the detectives Hirth, Fichtl, and Schulz; as for the other characters and for the plot, S. is free to invent them at will. It appears as if S. has set furiously to work, when in reality he's concocted a diabolical plan. I write: Instead of writing, S. has his friend, the arms dealer Proksch, instruct him in the proper handling of the latest model Glock; then the author stakes out a place to lie in wait, and he waits . . . and, to the horror and outrage of millions of television viewers, just as Detectives Hirth, Fichtl, and Schulz are leaving so-called Security Headquarters, he takes aim and shoots.

No, I write, I'm going to cross that out; it's a good idea but it's not true to life. *Something for the masses*, something *ordinary*, was what the director told me, Schmidt, that he wanted-ed. In England I go by Smith, by the way, Jolyon Brettingham Smith, something for the masses; but when I'm working in Lebanon, Schmidt's the other guy and I go by Cordes, or Korbes. The content is more important than the form, the director said, you'll come up with something.

It's after midnight. The rain beats against the windows. I

write: It's after midnight. It's stopped raining. I'm at the scene of the crime, hunched over the traces of an ordinary life. Notes lie scattered in front of me. Murder-suicide / after an argument / in Jenbach. Something's happened in this kitchen, I don't understand it. The pool of blood would seem to indicate tragedy. With this pistol, the police officer shot dead his ex-fiancée. A broken engagement. Pictures from their vacation together. *The Last Slide Show.* —So we've got blood, but how about suspense? And the suspect a policeman? I don't know. On the other hand, what was happening in the policeman's head, that would be interesting to find out, wouldn't it? *Policeman's head, interior, darkness.* Policeman's head. Interior. Darkness, disturbance, death. An interior view of the culprit, before and after, roughly:

11:10 P.M.: *Policeman's head, interior.* Pictures of their last vacation together. Beach scenes in Tunisia.

11:17 P.M.: *Policeman's head, interior.* Anger, grief, outrage.

11:21 P.M.: *Policeman's head, interior.* Pain, sadness, fury. *Down, strumpet! (Othello)*

11:26 P.M.: *Policeman's head, interior.* The phrase *I can't take it anymore* appears on the screen, in newsprint, clipped from a suicide note that had been published in the paper in the context of another homicide investigation.

11:27 P.M.: *Policeman's head, interior.* Resolve, split-second planning, preparing for execution.

11:31 P.M.: *Policeman's head, interior.* Electromagnetic impulses, commands from the brain to the eyes, hand, finger.

11:32 P.M.: *Policeman's head, interior.* Darkness, death. Light advances down the barrel of the gun, light at the beginning of the tunnel, *Light at the Beginning of the Tunnel,* could that work? No, I write, no, not like that. How then? *Adventures in the Oral Cavity? The Cold-blooded Pole?* (With this gold watch the perpetrator lured the child . . .) *The Naked Clown?* (With his face hidden behind this clown mask, the fiend assaulted the two young boys—? With this video camera his accomplice filmed the perversions—? While forcing the brothers to perform abominations of the most despicable sort, the intruder calmly helped himself to the younger boy's birthday cake [arrow points to cake]—? The pervert couldn't restrain himself, couldn't even keep his hands off the boys' coin and stamp collections—? With the words, *My name is Schmidt, I'm here for the rent*, the criminal smooth-talked his way into the boys' home—? The notebook: where a dozen victims' names were already listed—? But our perpetrator had not reckoned on the *competence* of detectives Hirth, Fichtl, and Schmalz—?) No, not like that. For the unenlightened masses, that's *nothing*. I write: Even were the rain beating against the windows, I would never write a thing like that.

If I were someone else, I'd have had something written by now. Someone else? Now there's an idea. *You've got a good idea there*, says Rolf Torring in *Adventures in the Oral Cavity*. I'll write some real *adventure fiction*, a real *Leo Frank* thriller, something gripping, something ripped from the headlines; and so that it doesn't lack for *humor*, I'll throw in a little realism, a little human emotion, a little of everything that goes into a genuine Leo Frank—*Alles klar, Herr Kommissar?* I may be no retired criminal investigator, but have I not written the sentence *Literature is a fight against crime?* There, see, I'm writing already. *Solo*, I write, by Leo Frank. Content: Prostitution kingpin Jelinek wants in on the arms trade. His bodyguard, the *Brute*, wants in on it too but is looking to run it *solo*. Three murders ensue. New paragraph. Detectives Hinterberger, Fichtl, and Schulz are put on the case but can't make heads or tails of it. Jelinek's faring no better. Then, single-handedly, Fichtl succeeds—, gets—, comes across—, discovers—, manages to—, finally succeeds in finding a clue and everything falls into place, everything falls into place. Good stuff. That should make a nice Leo Frank. I write: Under the glow of my lamplight, I'm rubbing my palms together. Now for a few details. Hinterberger, Fichtl, and Schulz take up the investigation. *Lots of ambiance.* An informer had given them the password for the arms deal, the sentence *My name is Schmidt, I'm here for the rent.* I write:

Vienna, 2nd District, Venediger Au Park, exterior, night.

Red Zora (*suggestively*): Four hundred. Seven if you want a golden shower.

Hinterberger: My name is Schmidt, I'm here for the rent. (*Softly*) The White Rose—what have you heard?

Zora: You talking about *Stinkhorn?* (*Whispering*) I don't envy that one, she got iced, says Flounder, fucked up the whole kitchen floor, nice new linoleum, too ... That's all I heard. *Cut.*

Arms dealer: Latest model Glock? We've got a gentleman's value pack, eleven for the price of ten, I'll throw in an extra magazine *gratis* ... This Glock here—

Fichtl: Name's Schmidt. I'm here for the rent ... (*Adding, under his breath*) What do you know about the shipment?

Arms dealer (*softly*): Careful, eyes are everywhere. Hotel Lucona, room twelve ... The shipment out of Israel's disappeared, the customers are already complaining. I'd find myself a *carpet*, if I were you, duty-free zone ... *Cut.*

Carpet warehouse, duty-free zone. The handoff takes place, it looks like the dealer will get away, maybe shot, maybe not. The dealer gets shot, but the investigator's screwed: the weapons are toy machine guns. Now, is that a genuine Leo Frank, or what? Oh yeah, that'll make a real nice Leo Frank. How did midnight come and go without my noticing? I write: How did midnight come and go without my noticing, I wondered, only to immerse myself again in my papers, my manuscript, insofar as one can speak of manu*script* and not manu*scrawl.* Onward, onward: *White Rose's funeral, exterior, day.* The Brute shows up with a gigantic wreath. Standing beside the open grave, moved to tears, soft-boiled Fichtl vows to bag the murderer himself. Quickly now, it's long after midnight, my temples ache, the hour of the wolf is nearing, onward. *Head of Inspector Fichtl, interior, darkness.* Wichtl cooks up a trap—*Fichtl,* pardon. Posing as an arms dealer, he lures the Brute to a vacant apartment. As soon as the password is spoken—*Abide with me,* was what they'd agreed on—wait: abide *what*—? What am I writing, *My name is Schmidt, I'm here for the rent, that's* the password. As soon as the password is spoken, Fichtl leaps out from behind the door and offs him. With his dying breath, the Brute confesses: Jelinek wanted in on the arms trade. I—now at last I can reveal my secret, in truth I'm not a Brute, my name is Schmidt—I didn't want to be a thug forever, I wanted to make something of myself, have something I could call my own. That three people had to die, well . . . that was an accident! Fichtl smacks the dying man and says with a laugh: *Good-bye, Mr. Schmidt* . . . Well, what do you think? That's how we do it south of the border, there you go, an *inimitable* Leo Frank!

I write: Rain beats against the windows; but I, in a state that can only be described as increasingly ecstatic, I'm already on to my next, even better Leo Frank thriller. My quill is literally flying across the paper. One content is as good as the next. I write: *The Passion.* By Leo Frank. The kingpin of the Roman Curia, under the strictest secrecy, wants in on the gambling and pornography trade. But his adversary, the archbishop coadjutor Schmidt, is planning to fleece his eminence's flock, so to speak. And so we come to some serious violations of the fifth and sixth commandments. Inquisitor Hirth, Father Fichtl, and the ecclesiast Schulz are to investigate the matter. It's only after a series of difficulties that Father Fichtl comes to a real *crossroads*, though in the end he manages to ward off the powers of darkness. Is that colossal or what . . . ? A genuine Leo Frank is versatile, exploits every trick in the book. And my next Leo Frank will be the best Leo Frank yet. *Once Upon a Sunday* . . . Content: Beggar King Jelinek and his accomplice, Asscheek Eddy, had staked out some Sunday newspaper boxes that no one had been patrolling. One Sunday, they nabbed them ... The petty-cash patrol officers Hinterberger, Fichtl, and Schulze, to their horror, assessed the damage at more than ten schillings, but beyond that were groping in the dark. It wasn't until the following Sunday, when they lay waiting in ambush, that they finally managed, after a wild pursuit, to capture and arrest the newspaper thieves ...

Morning nears. My pen hurries over the page! Burglar King Jelinek wants in on the arms trade then gets shot in the back. His buddy, the *Boor* ... Textile King Jelinek wants, for whatever reason, to get into the chocolate business. In the attempt, he crashes rather unluckily through a shop's skylight, severs his jugular, and bleeds to death. His attorney, *Mr. Boorman* ... Now this is what I call writing! Erlking Jelinek wants into the ballad business ... Kingfisher Jelinek wants into the music business. His agent ... The poet-prince Jelinek ... into the business of mass entertainment ... His rival, Peter Turrini, alias Rolf Torring ... the rights to the screenplay ... to land the ... it so happens that ... Hirth, Fichtl, and Schulz ... a mystery ... dead ... the deed ... the scene ... death ... the tie-in.

I write: It's morning. The rain has stopped. My business here is done. The rain has stopped. I shut off the lamp. There's a knock at the door. My name is Schmidt, comes a voice from outside, I'm here for the rent.

It was after midnight. No rain to be heard. On the tracks under the window, on a sidetrack, a diesel locomotive stood, had been standing for a while, engine idling, headlights dimmed, though it made no show of intending to depart. In the cheerless light of the cabin I saw a man holding papers in his left hand, instructions maybe, to which he kept referring before bending over some sort of equipment he then began fiddling with, with his right hand. Later I saw him sitting down, his head and upper body bent over a desk or some other such surface. It looked, under his little pool of lamplight, as though he was making notes or entering data on a form; then again, he could just as well have been reading an Edgar Wallace whodunit, who knows. Then the cabin suddenly went dark, though the engine kept on idling.

A pair of beat cops were strolling down the deserted street on the other side of the railroad embankment, the broad arc of their flashlights scanning the sidewalk as they disappeared around a corner. A man with a lantern came walking along the tracks; he wore a raincoat with the collar turned up and a hat fastened under his chin by an elastic band. Without missing a step, he bent down low, shined his lantern under the locomotive, then climbed the few steps to the cabin door and knocked on the window. He was let in right away and the cabin light came back on. The man in the raincoat, gesticulating with both hands, seemed to be speaking rather insistently to the locomotive driver, who in turn made quite a show of raising his left arm to expose the wristwatch under his sleeve and now stood glancing from his watch to his visitor, nodding like a man receiving and understanding instructions. Then the late-night guest, no, the early-morning visitor, since it was long after midnight by now, descended the stairs, and the locomotive driver let his arm fall and turned out the light. The other man—was this *The Sinister Man?*—walked away in the rain, the same way he had come. Suddenly a scream tore—

It's night. Rain beats against the window of the cell. In the hallway outside the cell there's a commotion: doors keep opening and closing again and locking, prisoners are taken for questioning and brought back again, sleep is unthinkable. How did I end up in this situation, what happened? I try to recall, I recall. It was very early in the morning, I crossed an empty street and approached a traffic sign to which a newspaper box was affixed, a self-service box. As I approached the newspaper box, I instinctively—subtly too, or so I hoped—scanned the street, eyes peeled for any inconspicuous persons seated in parked cars or peering out from behind half-drawn curtains in the apartment windows above me. I had to admit that all of a sudden I wasn't so sure whether this newspaper box wasn't—I'd been reading in the paper now for months about the threat of a widespread campaign—under surveillance by some secret service-like organization whose purported authority and punitive scope were not, as they say, on the books, and even if they were, then only as violations themselves. Fuming to myself, I neglected to even pretend to drop a quarter into the slot before angrily snatching a paper from the plastic box and moving along, or attempting to move along, but alas, it turned out otherwise. Somewhere behind me, though not too distantly, an engine was gunned, a car drove past then pulled up next to me, tires squealing, it all happened very fast. Two men leapt from the car, yelling something about newspaper surveillance before seizing me with their well-trained mitts. But I was able to wrench myself free and make a run for it, with the two of them running after; the third man, the driver, waited in the car. My chance of escape was looking good, or so I thought, when from a side street where I'd seen no one in pursuit, there came a voice: Stop! I'm armed! Stop right where you are! I slowed down and looked around, and in actual fact there was a fourth man standing there with his legs wide, gripping his gun, which he had pointed in my direction, with both hands. (I later learned it was a plainclothes officer who'd only incidentally happened along to head off my escape.) Meanwhile the other two had caught up with me, men in hats and coats, pinned my arms behind my back, and stuffed me into the backseat of their car. To headquarters? asked the driver, gunning the engine. Yeah, to the holding pen, replied the patrolman to the left of me. Lucrative day today, think there's even enough space for all our new friends? The other one produced a sound almost impossible to describe, which, I can only assume, was meant to be a laugh or a snicker of agreement. At headquarters, to which these henchmen led me through a courtyard — "General Security Administration for Print Media," read a small chalkboard next to the door — I was taken first to a *Gruppenführer*'s office for questioning. This bureaucrat — like all repulsive individuals, he wore a maroon-colored sweater-vest — paced in very deliberate circles around his desk while speaking with me, so that he appeared one minute in front of me and the next behind me. Name, he asked. My name is Schmidt, spelled *dt*, I answered. Oh, and you're probably here for the rent, he said with a sinister laugh before smacking me. If that's how you want it, we'll call you Schmidt then, but let this be a warning, Mr. Schmidt, to you and everyone else toying with committing this particular offence, an offence that for far too long now, don't ask me why — theft is theft, crime is crime — has been regarded as *minor*. This is a wrong that can only be righted by means of exemplary punishment. And we're well equipped here to purge you of your impulses. Another smack. Robbing a harmless, unarmed newspaper box, why it's worse than stealing an old lady's purse, far worse! But our organization is prepared to educate you in the proper handling of your Sunday paper. For, come rain or come shine, come stormy weather — are you listening to me, Mr. Schmidt? asked the Ober-, pardon, the Gruppenfüh-

ute more. *Crusade Against Newspaper Theft a Success! Media Saturation: Sensory Overload?* the loudspeakers shouted. *Addiction: A Modern Epidemic?* Enquiring minds want to know about: *Mass Shooting in* —; *Torture: Mock Execution in* —; *Terror: Unrest in* —; *Asset Seizure: Raid on* —. The headlines screamed: *Bull Tramples Child to Death. On the Slopes: One-legged Amputee Assaults School Children. Broken Leg in Unterinntal. The End is Near. Peter Lorenz: That's What They've Made of Him. Hell on Oedt.* Shouting and raging from every direction: *How Does Heinz Konsalik Do It? When Will Andrei Sakharov Return? Where is Patty Hearst? What to Make for Dinner in Under Fifteen Minutes? Newspaper Thieves: For Whom the Bell Tolls. Husband Stabs Wife! Wife Stabs Husband! Why Schleyer Must Die. Does Julius Hackethal Want Us to Die? Grass Terminally Ill? Are Germans Going Extinct? An End to the AIDS Crisis? Kohl: Where To Next? Euthanize the Elderly? Murder! Mayhem! Terror! Sex!* the speakers cried out. *How Does Rambo Do It? Falco's Bedroom Manner. The* Lucona *Sinks! Iran-Iraq: Battle Rages On! Horrifying Images of* . . . And so on and so forth . . . *Blackout!*

When I came to again, I found myself back in this cell, and here I am still. How I got here from the basement, I don't know. Rain beats against the cell window. What's that? There's a sound outside the cell, the doors are unlocked, a fellow sufferer is thrown inside.—This is absolutely unbelievable, the man stammers, absolutely unbelievable, I never would have thought it possible . . . Did they do to you what they did to me? Yes, I say, probably.—They abducted me, from my very own home, from within my own four walls, imagine that! I can hardly wrap my mind around it even now . . . Picture this: I'm sitting relaxing in my own living room, it's afternoon, I'm drinking a cup of tea and reading the paper I picked up earlier, in fact I happen to be reading, much to my amusement, a full-page notice about how dangerous the so-called print-media patrol is meant to be, comprised

of men culled from every social class, men you don't want
to mess with. An engineer, one Mr. Dietmar A., I read, was
contentedly reading a Sunday paper he hadn't paid for when
suddenly three patrol officers show up at his front door, I'm
reading the sentence, *In a flash he weighed his options*, and I
burst out laughing, then it sounds to me like the doorbell's
ringing, and it *is* ringing, I think, there it is again, insistently. So I open the door, newspaper in hand, and standing there
are two rather shabby though hefty figures, brandishing what
look like homemade badges of some sort, and they're shouting: Petty-cash Patrol!—I don't understand, I say good-na-
turedly, I don't keep petty cash around the house, since you
never know—case in point—who's going to show up at your
door. And with reference to their badges—badges indeed!—
I say a bit facetiously: when I was a kid, I was an altar boy,
and to show that I'd mastered the altar service, another boy,
the head altar boy, presented me with an *Altar Boy Certifi-
cate* he'd made himself, complete with stamp, seal, and signa-
ture, a document not unlike your own badges, Gentlemen, if
you catch my drift . . . Then I remember the theme song to an
old radio program, which seemed even more *apropos* of the
circumstances, *you* remember Hirschbold's *Achtung Sprachpo-
lizei!* I'm sure, so I'm about to start singing, *Look out, look
out, the Language Police!* when the one guy snarls at me: Muz-
zle it! And all of a sudden they push me back into my apartment and close the door behind them and allege: You put a
button in the coin slot of the a newspaper box, we've got you
red-handed, we know *everything.*—I'm telling you, my cell-
mate tells me, every Sunday for years now I've been putting
a button into that coin slot. My mother, God rest her soul,
passionate seamstress that she was, left me so many buttons
they'll last me years yet.—Yes, and I say to the men, such a
button falls directly under the rubric of a pittance, as does the
amount you exact in exchange for your news, if you catch—
A smart-ass and a scholar, one guy bellows and punches me

in the gut. Five hundred, cash, and we'll call it even, says the other guy, five hundred or you're coming with us! What?! I yell. Are you insane? Coercion, extortion, home invasion, and now you want to rob me of my freedom, all for a pittance? Sounds about right, comes the reply, theft is theft. I guess we'll just have to take the bounty for this one, the one guy says to the other, a lucrative day today! And by that point they've taken hold of me with their nasty media-patrol fingers, with their filthy mitts, and have hauled me down the stairs to their car and brought me here, to headquarters, or so I hear, and of what goes on here you're already aware . . . Oh, these newspaper crooks, he spat out the words, and their *self-serving* henchmen . . . Laying traps and molesting respectable people! Have you noticed meanwhile the way people are walking around now on Sundays, how they're always looking over their shoulders and acting cagey . . . ? But what am I supposed to do? Quit reading the paper? That's no laughing matter, it's a matter of having nothing to laugh at. And if I pay the amount in full — *in full*, what does that even mean? — I couldn't look myself in the face. And so I put my button in the slot, and now I've been kidnapped and tormented . . . Unbelievable, I mean it's incredible. — Anyway, have you thought about escape? No, I had to admit. Well, then, let's get out of here. . .

. . . Let's get out of here, my name by the way is Torring, my comrade said, Rolf Torring, and offered me his hand. I shook it heartily. Hans, I said, a pleasure. We'll call for the guards then knock them out, Rolf suggested; you, Mr. Hans, take the one on the right, I'll take the one on the left. Done and done. We took the keys from the guards and locked them in the cell. Then we sped cautiously through the passages, using niches and ledges as cover. On the ground floor we climbed out an open window and found ourselves in a courtyard. We gulped the fresh air into our lungs. It had meanwhile stopped raining.

It's

In front of me

I

yes, what was it I wanted, actually? Now I've forgotten. Wait, it occurs to me again, *I don't remember*, that's the line I'd been meaning to write. Hadn't I meant to start a novel, working title *Hero of the Opening Line?* —I, Christian Waldhammer, awoke one morning with bloodstained hands; next to me lay a naked woman, motionless, a kitchen knife stuck in her back. I couldn't remember a thing. *No.* —One night I, Anne-Sophie Mutter, collapsed right in the middle of the opening movement of Brahms's violin concerto in D major. *No.* —I am the Redeemer; suffer the common people to come unto me, that I might quicken them with magical fire and balloons. *No, not on my typewriter!* —I, Lorenz Fischer, was sent with the others to Soest to preach the Münsterite doctrine and to bring aid. Our calls for penitence rang through the streets, as we burst fearlessly into the councilor's chambers, where he was busy with affairs of state. But the councilor had us seized and ordered our execution. On the 23rd of October I was decapitated. *No.* —I, Tibor Foco, former European motorbike champion, future king of the underworld, whacked the whore Elfi over the head with a gear shaft then finished her off with a pistol shot. Afterward I relaxed and gave Regina a little taste of the best cock in all of Linz. But I remember none of it, except for the blowjob, and surely that's no crime. *No.* —Once upon a time, I, Herr Korbes, returned home to the nastiest surprise of my life. *No.* —My bad luck, the bad luck of Franz-Josef Murau, began the day I bought a book by Thomas Bernhard. *No.* —I, Georg Hauptfeld, a bachelor, seek prose of any kind wherein I can take a leading

leaned back. Behind me, close behind my head, I heard three men speaking, quarreling it seemed over a peculiar matter. — A hero should never be passive, one was just saying, a hero has to have contours, particular habits, particular props, even a particular setting will do; a maroon-colored sweater-vest isn't enough, in any case. Have you read me in *Old Masters*? I'm sure you've read me in *Old Masters*, it was my most iconic role, as they say ... Sitting on the settee in the Bordone room of the Kunsthistorisches Museum, my cane wedged between my knees ... Let the violent rhetoric, the tirade of abuse, let the poetics of the table of judgments commence! I need only say: This country is a cesspool of ludicrousness, or: Each morning we blush in the face of such ludicrousness; and for the German literary critics, for *Die Zeit*'s Michaelis or these other idiots at the *Frankfurter Allgemeine*, I forget their names, it's like a revelation, the literary world is *aghast*. I need only make an appearance, saying: You live in a thoroughly ludicrous and, in truth, an utterly depraved world — *What annihilating fury!* The entire world of today is a ludicrous one, that is the truth — *What denunciating fervor!* How can such a pretty landscape mask such an abysmal, moralizing mire — *The art of the fugue! Here is an author writing his way unwaveringly into world literature!* Of course it's a pleasure to be the hero of such a highly esteemed book, and the perfect incompetence of the sycophantic press — what's it to me? Each sentence put on the page, into my mouth, each tell-all all-censuring hence telling of nothing and utterly indifferent sentence is received with gratitude, showered with acclaim, can a character ask for anything more? *Signs and significance*, my dear Atzbacher — yes I know, esteemed colleague, your name is not Atzbacher but I can call you that if I like — signs and significance! This is art's insoluble problem, is it not? The sign and its significance must be unanimous, yet the sign is not the significance! Signs and significance, the *poetics of the table of judgments*! Dear Atzbacher, or shall I call you

Frank?—Ah, but the trick then is not to describe the ordinary in an extraordinary way, another voice broke in, rather to describe the extraordinary in an ordinary way, this too is important: an extraordinary hero clearly described, put plainly on the page. *It stank! It stank!* No doubt you don't recognize me—I was depicted a bit differently in the book—but surely you've read me as Grenouille in *Perfume*, an extraordinary and extraordinarily successful hero, yet with the humblest, most common of means. *It stank, it stank*, ha ha! The rivers stank, the marketplaces stank, the churches and the palaces stank—this is how the scene, how the playing field is laid for a successful hero! The streets stank of manure, the courtyards of urine, the stairwells stank of rat droppings and the kitchens of rotten cabbage—it's that simple . . . The parlors stank—like that, do you understand? The stench of sulfur rose from the chimneys and the stench of lye from the tanneries; from the slaughterhouses came the stench of blood and from mouths the stench of rotting teeth—superb, wonderful! A magnificent setting for a hero, albeit one in which I have to hold my nose; a rewarding role nonetheless. The peasants stank, the priests stank, the whole of the aristocracy stank, that's how it's done, if you want your book to succeed! Or like this: The air was heavy with the sweet scent of sweat and lust—how beastly and lush! The extraordinary described in an ordinary way: gazes stumbled madly over this landscape of straddling flesh! *They copulated*—the voice kept on, increasing in both fervor and volume, as the waiter passed, his jaw set—*they copulated*, groaning, grandfather with virgin, apprentice with nun, Jesuit with day laborer, all topsy-turvy, just as opportunity presented!—Gentlemen, please tone it down, came the waiter's voice, there are other patrons present! Tone it down? asked the voice that was calling itself Grenouille. What are you talking about? I heard every word you said, the waiter replied. You heard nothing, the older voice interceded, nothing is what you heard! Signs and their signif-

It's midnight. Wrong, it isn't midnight at all, it's afternoon, a hot mid-afternoon in mid-April: *writing desk, interior, day,* the windows are open.—It was, thus, a cold February night. I was hungry. No, that's a lousy beginning. No access here to anything original. This heat! The radio is doing a feature on Naples, a collection of acoustic postcards broadcast in the sonorous voice of a journalist by the name of Schlock, *An Italian Journey,* by Goethe Schlock—useless, I think; heavy traffic, too much noise, too much shouting, just like Naples. Too much shouting, too much noise, coming in through the window, coming out of the radio; sure I could turn the radio off, but should I turn the radio off just because the program's stupid? I could also close the window, but why should I close the window when the idiots out there could just as well, no, could better yet, yes, should, best of all, stop polluting the air with their cars?—Where then to begin, and how? I've been back there—but where? In Nieder-Eschbach, Bonames, on Konrad Duden Way? As a virtuoso chamber musician, I travel quite a lot, but in Bonames, on Konrad Duden Way it was not, not this time; not like back then, the view from a highrise apartment on an afternoon in early fall, overlooking Nieder-Eschbach, the outlook rather grim.—No, it could have been a motel on the North Atlantic coast, or was it, here I'm never certain, an American military base on the banks of the Main? I must have come often to this motel, but my memory of it is dim. At the gas station that doubled as the reception desk, I bought beer; the pump attendant, doubling as the bellhop, was watching a soccer match on a small TV that sat on the counter, and was annoyed by the interruption. I crossed both the courtyard and the parking lot, which were one and the same, on my way to my room. There was a housekeeping cart on wheels standing next to the door to my room; I noticed a decal on the trash can, a talking hedgehog holding some kind of flag, maybe the German flag? One flag's as good as the next. And what did the hedgehog have to say? *Error!* said the hedgehog, as he climbed down the toilet brush? *I'm pro-defense*, said the hedgehog, staying put on the trash can. I'm in favor of making ready for defensive warfare, says the plastic German trash can; *Nuremberg, Nuremberg, du bist ein ausgeleerter Kübel*, this old song came into my head as I surrendered myself to my drab little cell inaptly termed a room. I sat down on the bed. I drank my beer from the toothpaste glass and my schnapps straight from the bottle, and thought about how I'd spend the evening that was falling fast, that was closing in on top of me. I wouldn't be spared the effort of leaving the room again since I'd have to find something to eat, more precisely: take in some nourishment. Now on the one hand, there was nothing I would have liked better than to leave this little room, with its peeling plastic wallpaper that appeared to be patched here and there with Band-Aids; on the other hand, there was nothing worse I could think of than having to return to the thoroughly hostile outside world. There's nothing so dreadful as traveling abroad and having to sit and eat alone in some restaurant—eat, don't make me laugh! Oh, Eva Ingeborg, Kristin, Lisi, why have you forsaken me tonight?! I went to the window and looked out: the window overlooked a small park and a restaurant, *PizzaLand*, according to the glaring neon sign. Land, ho! someone else may have shouted, PhotoLand! Carpet-Land! TombstoneLand! PizzaLand! But me, would I ever find a plot of land I might claim as my own? I hesitated, my hunger was still well under control. I couldn't tell whether the restaurant was occupied, whether PizzaLand was densely populated or not; though by the way the waiters and bussers were rushing around one was tempted to conclude that business was booming. I sat back down on the bed and tried to come

one must wait his turn in line, until he's called, invited to come in. I dreaded and was also relieved to think that nothing might come of my little table for one. In rapid succession—any more rapidly and it would have played out like a silent film—guests, American soldiers for the most part, left the restaurant, crossed the barricade, while new guests lined up behind me. All the while waiters kept coming to the barrier and calling out into the crowd: Three, *drei*, or four, *vier*, which meant they had an open table with either three or four seats, before quickly disappearing again inside the restaurant, with the lucky seat holders following. Other guests exited the restaurant holding to-go boxes with pictures of telephones printed on them and the inscription *PizzaPhone*. I approached the barricade and asked a waiter if I could order a pizza to go. He invited me to follow him to the register and handed me a menu, I picked the first name I saw, Margarita (and now this too: I'll never be able to fall in love with a woman by that name!), and the waiter asked me: Last name? First? I was caught so off guard by these sudden questions that I told him my real name: Christoph Willibald Gluck. I paid—on the bill he'd written only my first name—and the waiter said: Twenty minutes! and sent me back to the vestibule to wait. I sat down on the bench and waited. Now, how to bridge the time?—Oh, it's so arduous assembling sentence after sentence about a cold February night on a far too humid afternoon at the end of April, the stagnant weather, winds out of the east, holding off the Mediterranean low-pressure front, an easterly wind, all's quiet, no cause for concern, I'm leaving the window open.—I pretended to read my magazine, interested enough to appear absorbed in the article if necessary and at the same time sufficiently bored to be able to look away if I wanted. Guests left, guests came, the number of those waiting remained the same. A lot of blacks were among them, entire families lined up for a meal that was meant to take as long to eat as the time spent waiting for it. Well—

well, well, well!—they're Americans, so-called US citizens, I said to myself, they're not used to having it any other way, and yet, to judge by the way they're dressed and the women's makeup there must be some pleasure in this for them, they wait so patiently, deliciously anticipating a meal that will only turn out a disappointment to them, I think; but that's just it: no one here's anticipating their expectations will be disappointed, it's the disappointment itself they expect to be fulfilled ... Oh, whatever, screw it, I couldn't care less about Americans, and soldiers at that; I don't give a damn about soldiers, let alone American ones. My penalty period must have ended since from the depths of the restaurant I heard my name being called: Mister Willibald or Herr Reinfried, whatever it was. I hurried over to whomever was calling me, showed my receipt, was handed a warm box and allowed to leave this PizzaLand—thank you, fresh air at last! Walking back to the motel I took a look at the imprint on the box: *PizzaLand* and *PizzaPhone*, including telephone cord and receiver. PizzaPhone! Hello, this is PizzaLand, who is calling, please? This is Processed Cheese, hello? Hello, Processed Cheese?! Processed Cheese, come in please.—I was back in the room by now, I'd long since dragged the table over to the bed, sat down on the bed, and torn open the box only to realize there had been no plasticware provided. So I sat tearing off hunks of the soggy crust with my fingers and stuffing them in my mouth; the so-called pizza looked and smelled like warmed-over, half-baked vomit. How convenient, I thought, to be spared the trouble of having to vomit later myself. I packed the remains of the pizza back in the box and threw the box in the trash, opened the window to air the place out, and went into the bathroom, washed my hands, and brushed my teeth. I passed the rest of the evening with beer and schnapps, listening to the radio—the device was built into the wall and offered a choice of three programs! At midnight—day, oh a new day at last, Sunday!—a symphony

In front of me stands a traveler. In front of him two travelers are waiting, and in front of them another traveler. In front of them three passengers are standing, and in front of them, at the counter, I can see a few members of a larger family or small clan — fat, short Indians, they have a lot of bags to check, a whole lot of bags, and there are difficulties, misunderstandings that need clearing up, and these things take time. And behind me travelers are waiting. Although I'm standing in a line, or rather because I'm standing in a line, I feel cornered. For if I fall, who will help me up? If I sway, who will steady me without any awkwardness ensuing, a crowd gathering, a rescue operation for which I'll be to blame, for which I'll have to pay; this way, there he is, the culprit, a victim of circulatory collapse, of an obsessive anxiety, of a mysterious illness, who wants to know? It'll be revealed in the course of the investigation, a victim of his own devising, in any case. I myself don't know, is it the alcohol, is it a sudden lack of oxygen to the brain? Places to sit are few and far between. How it is these people can remain on their feet, in front of me, behind me, in the neighboring lines, as if it were the simplest, most obvious thing in the world, incredible. Don't stagger, don't fall, I tell myself, I'm still standing, I'll pay no heed to my weakness, to my dreaded fatigue, I have to reach my destination, my writing desk, my radio on top of it, my papers that read *I traveled to Germany to experience something. It's midnight. Behind me, the tourist.* But how will I reach my destination when there are so many others in front of me likewise struggling, with increasing difficulties, to reach their destinations, albeit they at least stand secure and as though it were self-evident on the ground of reality, unaware of the real difficulty there is in standing on two feet and nothing to hold on to. *Walking* upright isn't a problem for me, well-heeled hiker, speedy pedestrian that I am, I generally escape most situations with ease, but having to hold myself upright while standing—what do you mean the Indians have finally got their luggage through check-in? hardly!—holding myself upright while standing is getting harder and harder for me, the more so since I try to make sure no one notices the effort it requires. What would people think, there's a man, not even drunk—and when have I ever been drunk? me? drunk?!—who can't even stand on his own two feet. But wait!—no, don't worry, I'm still standing, but the line's moving now, there's been a breakthrough in negotiations at the counter, another close call but it seems I'll manage to escape once again.

Arrived, returned, no relief.

Diagonally overhead, on the desk—wait a minute, *overhead, on* the desk? Processed Cheese, please come in, Hermann Burger, please note, here again an opportunity presents itself for another *critical comment* in the *Frankfurter Allgemeine*, something along the lines of: So where then exactly—overhead or on top of the desk?—overhead, then, on the *top shelf* of the desk, there's a radio, a device manufactured by Kapsch, this model's called "Chorale." Lately, whenever I turn the thing on, every hour on the hour, a dull thud sounds and a sonorous voice admonishes: *Think of your heart!* (Am I hearing this right, I wonder, since this cautionary, funereal voice could just as well, *thud thud thud*, advise I *be prepared* or *be alert*, if I *see something, say something, the Führer is speaking* or *the Enemy is listening*, but the voice, knock knock knock, warns: Think of your heart. Aha, I think, a campaign, but campaign isn't exactly right, a public service initiative by the Ministry of Public Health and Education, broadcast via the Vienna public airways, that's more like it.) Think of your heart! I think nothing of it, is my first thought, though reflexively I reach out to put a stop to this artificial radio-heart, then I freeze and let my arm fall. Fine, I accept the challenge. I have nothing to hide, I tell myself, my heart is pure; if I refused to listen to this, it would probably be because I had good reason to avoid it, and that would be bad. The fact that I do sit and listen to this morbid warning several times a day is proof enough there's nothing I'm repressing as far as my heart is concerned; for that which is repressed—and turning off the radio would indeed be an act of repression—sooner or later erupts, perhaps in the form of cardiac neurosis, which, as yet, I've been spared. So I'll be quieted by this disquieting thought. And when through the ether the challenge sounds, I'll be prepared and keep my heart in mind. Of course the broadcast command is not that I keep it in mind, precisely, but I can only think of my heart if at the same time I've got it in mind, otherwise I won't understand, a twofold burden that in turn increases the risk of infarction. Once I actually did turn the radio off, the thud just sounded too ominous, and immediately I felt a pain radiating from my left shoulder, through my chest, and into my neck, which frightened me so badly I actually thought I was having a heart attack. I've listened obediently ever since. It's wonderful, isn't it? The heart beats seventy times per minute, I learned that from the radio; I've not yet counted along, it's always too noisy, but I'm sure that's the case. I have however discovered this: *The more I think of my heart, the harder it beats back.* Yes, I should really be more active, get more exercise, but then again maybe I shouldn't, since I've heard that athletes, due to their higher thresholds for pain, tend to suffer silent heart attacks. Just when I'm feeling well again, after months of this radiophonic heart condition, I learn that feeling well is exactly what I ought to be wary of, because the heart can silence its own attack. (*The heart keeps silent,* and not because it's bound to respect confidentiality of any kind, it just keeps silent, out of malice or out of stupidity.) I feel fine, I run up the stairs to the third floor to my heart's delight; everyone else only takes

It's mid-March.

There's snow on the writing desk. The entire edifice, the lamp, the radio, is hung with icicles, and winter's been over ten days already, the most bitterly cold winter in living memory. And the outlook is grim. The northeast European high pressure zone continues to drive continental cold-air masses against my writing desk, against its peaks and inner Alpine depressions, and confined atmospheric disturbances will only result in more snowfall. I did actually clear my typewriter of snow, it's in working order, only I'm so exhausted, I've nothing left to leverage against this visitation. Woe to the warbler who is just now migrating from the south.

It's storming. I scale the writing desk.

It's midnight. In front of me, in the lamplight, lies the questionnaire—a worksheet for compiling a *schedule of assets.* Wind rattles at the windows. I read: The liable party hereby affirms the information listed below is accurate and complete. Ha! Me, who is liable to no party, as the liable party, good one! *List your assets.* I read, *Do you have cash?* As if I had any cash. *Securities, savings bonds, pawn tickets?* What, is my name Süskind? *Jewelry and other valuables, expensive furniture, watches, chains?* Who do I look like, Konsalik? Utta Danella? Yeah, I have a chain, it hangs from the door to my apartment and I latch it every night to make it harder in the morning for the process server to barge in. *Electric kettles, razors, irradiation lamps?* Electric kettles, razors, *irradiation* lamps, give me a break, like I'd ever own anything of the sort. *Clothing, hats, shoes, umbrellas, canes?* Clothing, yes, and hats, shoes, an umbrella, even a cane, made of hazelnut wood, I carved it myself, with a polished metal knob on top, I take it hiking, it's a walking stick, though it makes a good weapon, which is something to think about should anyone think of confiscating it. *Ski equipment, canoes, sporting goods?* Funny. Ridiculous, actually. *Motorcycles, ATVs, speedboats?* Are you insane? What's next? *Televisions?* I knew it, and *no* is my astounding and unwavering response, as I've said before: I'm not stupid. *Weapons?* Several typewriters of various calibers; a pocketknife with a lockable switchblade that I picked up in Italy and smuggled across the border in a car belonging to my cousin, the judge, with his full awareness and consent; and an MG 42 in immaculate condition and fully operational, mounted by the window. *Cases, bags, baskets?* Two so-called Helsinki baskets and a couple of media cases, among them an elementary school

War and *On Dissent*, these are no longer worth mentioning? Who's asking? Are you some sort of judge? And how's a judge meant to have any knowledge of this sort of thing anyway? Well, judges can be unpredictable, and they're certainly persistent. Remember that time you were summoned to court for questioning, accused of having taken movable property not belonging to you, and there was something to do with whether or not you'd ever set foot in a particular attic, and even though you said from the start that you had never set foot in that attic, still the judge bothered to ask: When were you last in that attic? And what was the last thing you saw in that attic? And did you return to the attic, after the fact? It was really only your ingenuity that brought the proceedings to a halt; but I do still sometimes think of those finely beveled rafters in that attic, how nicely they would have burned in your, in my, in *our* furnace, the warmth they'd have brought to a chilly winter's night, but that's— Enough, quit blathering, it's long after midnight. But a person prone to daydreaming, a man who sleeps all afternoon, who's made the night his private day, that's a person who'd— And moreover, how's a judge meant to come by such a comprehensive socialist education anyway? Be quiet! There. Already forgotten. What? Exactly: I don't know anymore. Continuing on. All these volumes of the *Peking Review*, the immortal fame of Comrade Zhu De of the People's Liberation Army, not worth mentioning? Ah, but it is. *Taking Tiger Mountain by Strategy*, wherein Geier's gang of bandits will be infiltrated from within and destroyed from without, and their leader taken prisoner? That, for sure. The tireless critique of unregenerate despots on the capitalist path, of the winds blowing in from the right? That, absolutely. The winds from the right . . . and who is behind them but that *blowhard* of a despot that allowed the jewel thief and colonial commodity broker Heller into this country, the latter just a new breed of the old colonialist gang-leader Geier? This *windbag* has done nothing but smear the great proletarian cultural revolution with shit!—And the underground zine *The Urban Guerilla Concept*, calling for the buildup of the Red Army Faction and taking up arms in the struggle? Been underground so long it's presumed dead by now ... *He that understands and does not act has not understood.* Socialism or barbarism? Man or beast? Who wants to know? I, Teufel and Langhans of Kommune 1, ask myself, Pope Thomas Bernhard II. Or would I rather be Alfred Döblin or Albert Ehrenstein this time? Oh, enough of these tired old jokes so late in the day, so late in the game, enough semantic pretense, impersonation, masquerades, by and starring Willi Forst. Where were we? Yes, man or beast. Socialism or barbarism. To make a clear distinction between us and the enemy—but when it seems the dividing line runs straight through me, or is it obliquely?—But the revolutionizing of the private sphere, the sublation of the monogamous couple, and the corresponding *fixation*? No longer worth mentioning. Oh! but back then—back then everything was different. Back then— All right, enough. *The libido is as unstable as it is fixated.* A fine theory, undisputed. Oh, but this is the theory, taken as a guide to proper conduct, that's gotten me into such trouble in the past. Once, in Paris— Enough! No more! The *long march through the institutions*? No one's returned from that. The *great refusal*? The great refusal, yes, back in the day, in Krems, at the annual conference of the Association of Catholic Academics, what a production that was! What a performance, in collaboration with my composer friend Comrade Zobl, Comrade Zobl was just then composing his *memento mori* for Wilhelm Reich, *Orgasms*, or ...? Yes, that's it, it was during our Krems days, which of course there weren't enough of to speak properly of our *Krems days*, but anyway it was back then. Now, instead of my reciting poetry, as arranged—an evening of *lyrical ballads* had been billed—we interrogated the Catholic academics about their sex lives, all before an eagerly convened audience. After the start of my billed recitation, we finished writing out our questionnaires, and then we grilled those Catholic academics, like I said, and how! We heard the Catholics out on fellatio and cunnilingus, on the sixth and eighth commandments, it was quite the hearing, quite the colloquium, most interesting ... We ought to be thrown in the lion's den, in the Schönbrunn Zoo, an old woman from Montevideo told us — the lion's den! (My looks, by the way, haven't suffered much since then — on the contrary. Cut it out, it's unseemly for a poet to be running around like a narcissist; he ought to work hard, like Grass — Help! Quit it! Quiet now.) We are the *Lumpenproletariat* among culture makers, the culture *Tupamaros*—? I'm finished with all that, I'm not a member of any group anymore, haven't been for decades. The avant-garde author as the ally of the local working class, enlightenment in the arena of mass entertainment? Not a chance. *Long live international solidarity*—? A meaningless incantation. And what about *associative delirium*, what was that about, back in the day? Well, the somewhat bewildered readers were calling for a clue to help them decipher my prose, and that's what they got: *associative delirium*.

Ah, what a schedule of discredits! Intelligibly formulated political engagement, ideological clarity, and what came of it? Nothing. Nothing but a handful of plants and animals got discovered, and that's it; a commitment to exploring new forms of life leaves us tracking the elusive corncrake, studying the marmot's lifecycle, watching it dry grass for hibernation and pace back and forth in front of its den, there you have it. — What's that? I ask my companion, whose father had fostered in her a specialized knowledge and appreciation of the varieties of plant and animal life, and with whom I, another man, now wander through the mountains year after year, asking *what flower is that?* That's violet rock flower. And that? Scarlet saxifrage. Violet rock flower and scarlet saxifrage! I shout, delighted; so as not to disturb the wildlife, I keep my shouting to the page, of course. And this here? I ask. Those are woolly headed thistles and wormwood. Woolly headed thistles and wormwood, if that don't beat all! I shout, clapping my hands. And down there? Wolfsbane! And up here? Forget-me-nots. You don't say, wolfsbane and forget-me-nots flowering here secretly still! And so much more yet to discover! Arnica, the herb renowned for its healing properties, columbine, and Turk's head lily, also known as the turban lily, the Scottish maple, and the wych elm! *Desire under the wych elms,* oh yes that too, if you know what I mean—from behind, while standing, bent over with hands pressed against a trunk. And cat's-ear, yes, and cat's ear. What kind of bird is that circling above us, I asked, buttoning my jeans, a golden eagle or a white-crested vulture? A white-crested vulture. Yesterday I watched a wood grouse burst chattering out of the thicket, and today a white-crested vulture watches us, and we watch him watching us, I shout, isn't this wonderful?!—Or here, this dusky, shady spot, rowan berries and holly, swamp brake and horsetail, badger droppings and the flattened underbrush where a fawn had been sleeping, profound peace, a very pretty little spot. Yes, this interests me. A weasel crossing my path on its way to drink from a nearby stream catches my attention. The serenity of the forests and meadows and valleys . . . *Before his hut, quietly in the shadows / Sits the ploughman, his hearth smoking, content,* this is the place I'm looking for, walking stick in hand. The woodpecker's labor, the song of the lark, this is what fascinates me, the economically profitless, commercially useless. For me there's more joy in ten carnations than in a hundred jobs in the tourism industry, or any industry at all. The forgotten history of the High Tauern gold mines concerns me more these days than does the history of Social Democracy; medieval guilds interest me more than the strike-breaking and racketeering trade unions of today. The highlands are nearer me than late capitalism is now. *The highlands in the age of late capitalism,* an essay, yet to be written . . .

Rain beats against the windows, harder now. In front of me, yes, there it is again, the schedule of assets. Part two: Claims. Do you have anything to claim, and from whom? Claims. A list of my claims would be nearly incomprehensible, my claims change constantly, from day to day, hour to hour, moment to moment, and yet they're always the same. I have nothing, I claim it all! Or is it that I have it all and nothing to claim? *Mortals live/By labor and wage, alternating labor and rest/And all is happiness . . . ?*—But if I must choose only a few, I claim the right to my pick among all the women and literature prizes in the world. Indeed, I love the speculative male gaze upon the female figure, women circulating in the marketplace; nothing's as thrilling as alienation.—As an early retiree, I claim compensation for the abuses I've suffered in this apartment—in this building, in this city!—for damages incurred as a result of the revulsion I experience living in it, and for the noise; a harassment settlement, reimbursement for the decades I've endured under this city's public housing administration! Of course I must also claim the resignation of the city's gloss-finish mayor, so loud, and always running around, screaming about how great this shit town is, which is to say that he's a liar, like all politicians, all small-time *consensus and rehabilitation* politicians whose resignations I likewise demand, as well as the immediate resignation of each of their designated successors, they're good for nothing and they're all the same, all the same, nothing but crooks, *nothing but crooks!* All they've got are one-track minds, concerned only with their own money and power, the main thing with these guys is they just want to *get in there* and *stay* there. And then there's this President of ours—out with him too! Muck this Midas stable clean, I demand the shit be shoveled, Carl Palla-

vicini, Vienna, 1st District! *Where do these claims originate?*
Where, indeed. Out of profound dismay and increasing
concern, extreme agitation, perplexity and alienation, out
of rage and sorrow, disgust and revulsion, pain, discourage-
ment, and sincere human sympathy, out of intense emotion-
al strain and heartfelt commiseration, out of outright provocation and growing indignation. *Do you have anything else
to claim, and from whom?* I claim that it is necessary for en-
ergetic action to be taken in the crackdown on drug-related
crime, in the battle against the trade, production, and con-
sumption of all narcotics, no matter the class, caliber, or engine capacity, in particular that an immediate halt be made to
automobile production and individual consumer use, that all
extant models be forthwith scrapped and all importers and
dealers dealt with in an exemplary fashion, I've been calling
for this for years! Two thousand annual drug-related deaths
on average in this country alone is two thousand too many,
not to mention all the other repercussions (all of them de-
structive) since space on this form is limited. My claim regarding the necessity of a ban on all so-called Alpine skiing
goes without saying. And, even still, my inventory of claims is
far from complete. I claim that it's past time for the uncondi-
tional withdrawal of NATO from Europe and the immediate
recall of HTLV-III, a gift to the world courtesy of the United States of America, a novel little CARE package, *from Dr.
Frankenstein with love, Fort Detrick, Maryland.* As for Reagan:
Let's bring a people's case / to Gaddafi's court for that shitface!
So goes the plea of my lonesome, sleepless nights! As for the
Nevada deserts, I claim that an immediate end must be put
to the ongoing provocation, to the subterranean nuclear ter-
rorism; I claim the right to a merciful earthquake, that it be
wrought upon us by a merciless nature — or better yet, that a
merci*less* earthquake be wrought by a merci*ful* nature, merciful and righteous. Accordingly, I have to claim, to *demand*
that Pitschek & Co., which runs its dubious little operation

out of the ground floor of my building, remove all American flags from its company vehicles, lest I be forced to do so myself. Yes, *hate*. Hate is good. *Where do these claims originate?* What? Oh yes, like I said, out of powerlessness, bitterness. Bitterness is hate fermented, powerlessness its vessel, if you'll allow me to—

It's out of powerlessness that I sit down to my desk to write and out of powerlessness that I get up and walk away again. Every hour on the hour I listen to the news in order to find out whether this or that one of my claims might have been met—but no, on the contrary! Must I always take matters into my own hands, I wonder. No, it's utterly hopeless: No amount of rain beating against the windows will help, not even if it were storming out like before, nor will the sunrise make any difference. No assets but incapacity. When the church bells tolling wake me in the afternoon—morning, by my calculation—all I'll be capable of doing is turning on the radio to find out whether the world's still spinning. What a way to start the day.

Been back there again. Saw it all, heard it all; the voices in the mail van in the afternoon making the tourists drowsy, the twilight-of-life stories, monotonous descriptions of car wrecks and hospital stays, accidents while bailing hay, *Here ended the wretched life of our dearly beloved Rupert Sabernig*; tales of late-night notifications, acquiescence to the facts, each has his own cross to bear; I've heard it all, where it took place, that the incoming call is from the police, *phoning it in*, that's how it goes around here; heard the rain was bitterly needed, heard the Törggele wine's bitter this year, heard it all and thought: *Thinking of childhood, like thinking of a previous life*, this line I've heard echoing in my own head, heard it all, voices in the mail van, phone calls and bird calls, the vulture's cry, the furious ibis, the song of the lark, of the sparrow, heard it all, seen it all; seen sycamore, elm, ash, wild cherry trees in the woods, watercress and water lilies on the riverbank, horsetail on the moor, snakegrass in the marsh, in the shade, I, Lenz, I've seen it all, in the mountains, on the way to my mill, to my goldmines, to the coal pile: *Before his hut, quietly in the shadows/sits the ploughman*, radiant days in June, in July, sunset, haze on the horizon, smoke rising from the cottages, *his hearth smoking, content*, I've seen larch and pine, juniper, violet rock flower and scarlet saxifrage, turban lily and wolfsbane, the gentian stood side by side with their bells upturned like a brass band, forget-me-nots, and deer tracks under the brush, Saturn glowing in the night sky, the pale blue of the moon looming over the darkened tree line, silhouetting the alpine ridge, seen it all before, and yet *my foolish request causes the magic to flee; darkness falls*, invisible shadows lie over everything.

Invisible shadows lie over it all: over castle and barn, mill and millpond, hamlet and hearth, shadows, imperceptible, over fields and plains, trees and hedges, over rocks and rock flowers and scarlet saxifrage, over cat's ear and lady's smock, shadows over dandelions, ragweed, and succulent clover, unseen over countless roses, unseen shadows over every thing that blooms after its kind.

And yet, I've seen nothing, heard nothing. The table's laid and yet empty. I've heard the rain, yes, but no vulture's cry, no furious ibis, no song of the lark or sparrow, not a sound from the kingfisher. I've heard nothing, seen nothing, in the woods, no wild cherry trees, no ash, elm, sycamore, no watercress on the riverbank, no horsetail on the moor, no fern in the shade; there's no way back to my mill, to my mill pond, no way back to my hamlet; only the menacing toll of bells welcome the wanderer to this deserted village. No gloaming I've seen, no haze on the horizon, no ploughman content to sit in the shadow of his hut; I've seen no violet rock flower, yellow either, no blooming elder, no forget-me-not, no turban lily, I've seen nothing, neither larch nor pine nor juniper, the holy shrub of the Celts.

I've seen nothing, not Saturn glowing in the night sky, nor the soft illumination of the moon rising over the ridge, behind the wood. I've seen it all and seen nothing. I've heard the rain. Never been there before.

together, that I'd ever been to before, I thought; I'll be sure to listen closely to the curator's commentary. He gave his name as Kurnitzky, by the way, and, sundry experiences with other Führers notwithstanding, I have no cause to doubt he's telling the truth. — So, let's begin with the Stone Age, shall we, he said as we entered a cool marble hall, since after all — if you'll forgive me the joke — no matter at what point we begin our journey through German history, sooner or later we're going to end up in the Stone Age. So, here we have our first *space-within-a-space* installation, the *sacred grove of the German musical arts*. We have to be quiet, the curator added, putting a finger to his lips. Laid out in row upon row were black pedestals on which rested plaster busts of German composers. I recognized right away the creator of *Palestrina,* Hans Pfitzner; the master of the fairy tale opera *Black Peter,* Norbert Schultze, whose charming opus I'd seen performed as a kid at the Klagenfurt City Opera house; and over there were Richard Strauss and Franz Lehár. Before a pedestal on which stood the bust of Anton Bruckner my Führer paused and stood, as if before a war memorial, in grim, impassive reverence, his hands folded over his belt, his service cap in hand. — In another part of the hall — this must be what they refer to as a multipurpose hall, since quite suddenly the scene changed — several men stood behind composer's desks, humming and singing to themselves, trying out melodies, running their hands absentmindedly through hair that by now stood nearly on end as a result, executing hand movements that were difficult to decipher, and making notations in pencil on sheet music; each appeared profoundly engaged in his work. — *Profundity* has always been the Germans' *forte,* the curator said in a whisper. Look over there — he pointed to a composer — Carl Orff envisioning the music to Shakespeare's *A Midsummer Night's Dream,* and there — he gestured at a desk nearby — you'll see Rudolf Wagner-Régeny at work at the same task. Next to him stands Cesar Bresgen, who is composing as we speak — my

Führer paused briefly and turned a scrutinizing ear in the direction of the man indicated, who didn't appear to be aware of us—yes, he's composing his *Funeral Rites* right now, it's coming along well; he's about to begin notation on his *Festlicher Ruf* for timpani and brass, though we won't have the privilege of hearing it, we ought to be moving along, German history is of *untold dimension*. Nevertheless, should you have occasion to visit the museum again, I recommend you time it so that you're here while he's composing his fanfare for brass—it's wonderful, I tell you, it's a thrill every time . . . And now on to the Egk section!—Here is Werner Egk at work on *The Magic Violin*, right now he's rehearsing a scene featuring Guldensack; at the desk next to this he's working on a piece commissioned by the Reich Broadcasting Corporation of Leipzig—just look at that: the profundity, the *effort!* It's a consecration-play, *Die hohen Zeichen*, after Weinheber, who's an Austrian, too, just like you, funny, isn't it? He'd best hurry, the broadcast premier is scheduled for the Führer's fiftieth birthday. Over there he's wresting from himself the *March of the German Youth,* and across the way you'll see— all of a sudden an entire band was there—the SS military corps band under the direction of Obersturmführer Schmidt, they're playing—listen, just listen to that!—a piece from Egk's ballet *Joan of Zarissa*. And now to our pièce de résistance! We arrived at four conductor's podiums, behind which four identical-looking men with hair like crested larks stood vigorously waving their batons.—The Aachen General Music Director von Karajan rehearsing *Celebration of the New Front* by Richard Trunk and Baldur von Schirach, the Führer exclaimed, a four part cycle for men's chorus and orchestra, thus the four podiums and the four conductors! The movements are as follows: first, *Hitler*; second, *The Führer's Guardians*; third, *O Country*; and fourth, *Horst Wessel*. An extraordinarily successful installation, don't you think?

Again the scene changed.—We're now approaching the

Writing Desk Collection, the Museum Führer explained, gesturing toward a vast collection of writing desks of all shapes and sizes.—A staggering *space-within-a-space* installation, a *colossal* environment, an *incessant* performance, as you're about to discover. Writing desks have always played an important role in German history, if not *the* most important; even Dr. Höfer's famous baby powder was invented at a writing desk! German civil servants—staggering in view of their competence, scrupulous in their performance of duty —have always enjoyed a great deal of respect from admirers and detractors alike. Let's take a quick stroll down the center aisle ... Ah, look at all these writing desks ...! Here, for instance, you'll find the desk of Dr. Kaltenbrunner, he's gone for a coffee break at the moment. Behind that writing desk there is Dr. Hanns Martin Schleyer, just look at him, so hard at work, incredible, isn't it? Show me the desk and I'll give you the man, as we say here in Germany ... And now here's a desk from the Ministry of Construction; the architect bent so industriously over his blueprints and maps—now he's leaning back thoughtfully in his chair, do you see?—this man is my father. Sadly, he passed away last year, leaving me nothing but boxes of blueprints for the reconstruction of the eastern territories; since then I've been working here as Führer.—Here is the desk of Lieutenant—the Führer needed a moment to think about it—Lieutenant or First Lieutenant Waldheim, he's away from his desk right now. This writing desk on the other hand, an especially lovely piece, belongs to one Lerch in Lublin, though at the moment he's also away, gone to fill in for his commanding officer, who has himself gone east to oversee the construction of furnaces. The writing desk of *his* commanding officer unfortunately has not been preserved; that's the man who signs off as Globotschnigg, by the way— another Austrian, what a coincidence!—Was this THAT Globotschnigg, my favorite mass murderer, I wanted to know ...—It's possible, replied the curator; in any event, the Austrians have always played a crucial role in German history, without the Austrians German history would be wholly unthinkable; even to this day, over and over, we find ourselves having to rely on the Austrians, as you'll see in a moment. So many writing desks, so many writing desks, I'm amazed every time ... — And that desk in the back there? I asked, pointing toward a remote part of the hall (it's possible it could have been another hall entirely) where, appearing as if out of a mist, I thought I discerned more desks. — Those are the desks of the poets and philosophers, the Führer replied, you can't always see them ... Yes, it's curious, actually: sometimes they seem very close and appear perfectly in focus, at other times they're obscure and remote, and still other times you can't see them at all. It seldom happens that they're completely indiscernible, though it happens more often than, say, a solar or lunar eclipse. Right now, though, the view is excellent, as if from atop a summit on a clear day, the curator continued. And in fact — the veil lifts — there the writing desks were, plain as could be, so close you could have reached out and touched them. Some were neatly organized, like the ones I'd been shown earlier, while others were home to an absolute mess as complex as it was chaotic, cluttered with writing utensils, notes, books, and sundry other objects, and it was among these untidy ones that — terror gripped me — I thought I recognized *my* writing desk; the longer I looked, the less I doubted — *that* was *my* writing desk! It was all right there, the armaments above, the rolltop rolled back, the heavy radio starboard on the upper deck, the lamp, everything in the exact order — *in the disorder that is my secret order* — in which I remember having left it: pencils and pens to the right of the old typewriter, notepad to the right of the chair on the wooden pull-out shelf that I used as a makeshift bar, and as a matter of fact there were my pilsner glass and the bottle belonging to it, my ashtray, a pack of cigarettes, my jerry-rigged Zippo, and a full glass of schnapps. What's more (I don't

ing them, invaded Germany, driving the Sudeten Germans *en avance*—look here, a Czech dagger from the era, note the savage curve of the blade. Under the flimsy pretext that the Germans were said to have attacked a Polish radio station, the Poles overran our borders in a *blitzkrieg*, despite the heroic statement from our chancellor that "as of 5:45 A.M. today, we have been returning fire." This Polish field howitzer testifies to the fact. From the north, the Danes and Norwegians didn't wait long before they attacked in turn, not least with a mind to plundering Germany of its vast mineral reserves. Here you'll see a Norwegian combat helmet, next to that a Danish cadet's pistol. On the 10th of May, 1940, Belgium, Luxembourg, and the Netherlands invaded Germany; we have here a Luxembourgian captain's uniform, a Belgian carbine, and a Dutch knapsack, all original documents of the day. I'm sure by now you've guessed or maybe you knew already that England and France realized it would be a mistake to miss out on the action. During the British air raid—here we have an RAF bomb—no real victories were decided, but the French had slightly better luck: on the 14th of June the Tricolore flew over Munich's Marienkirche and French troops were marching through the Victory Gate to the Feldherrnhalle. Bavarians wept openly in the streets, as these photographs here attest. But worse was yet to come. Fearing war, Hitler made a pact with Stalin. When diplomats reported back that Stalin was planning to invade Germany, Hitler lent it no credence. And so it happened that the Russian and Near East forces met with little to no resistance as they marched into Germany at the end of June, 1941. This is how, in those days, Germany became an increasingly multiethnic state. As if that weren't enough, Jewish conspirators *in their own country*, under whom we'd already suffered so bitterly, summoned Greek and Yugoslav partisans, Gypsies, too, and sundry other riffraff, to come and claim a share in the spoils. Come on in, come on, there's plenty to go around, it seemed the Jews were announcing around the world; even North Africans were making ready to claim a piece of the German pie. Here we have the torn panties of a young German woman who was raped by a North African, and there you'll see the blood-soaked uniform of a German soldier who was shot in the back by partisans. This photograph shows a clan of Gypsies roasting a suckling pig over a campfire in the middle of the state rooms of a villa they sacked in Garmisch-Partenkirchen, a villa that once belonged to Richard Strauss.—Now we're approaching the gallows. The gallows recall Germany's bitterest days. *Death by hanging.* This was the disgraceful sentence pronounced over and over again by the terror courts of the occupying forces. Many great German men—preeminent captains of industry, gifted military leaders, upstanding civil servants, and competent, dedicated doctors—were shown no mercy. Millions upon millions of Germans were deported or murdered in extermination camps, millions more are living in diaspora to this day. Yes, our people were dealt an unfair hand, but we never lost faith. Now, the real turning point in this genocidal war against Germany came when the Americans got involved. At first Germany feared the Americans were in it only to claim their share just like all the others, but the purported enemy soon proved itself a friend. In the firebombing of Dresden that followed, the Americans managed to thoroughly confuse the Russians, and they swiftly drove out most of the other invading forces as well. To this day, we keep them around out of gratitude, as our welcome and benevolent rulers; *that* is the truth.—That's the reason, then, for all the American radio programs, for this blossoming of American culture in your country, I say appreciatively, so that's how it all came about.—You understand me very well, the Führer replied, which is a rarity these days, like I said.—So that's how it all came about, I said again, thank you very much for your lively recitation.

It's midnight. Rain beats against the head that is bent over the writing desk. In front of me, the curator. Behind me, the tourist; he thinks, I write. I write:

These are very peculiar installations, my Führer said with satisfaction as we strolled through the halls that housed the extermination camp installations, very peculiar ... A space-within-a-space installation like the one you're about to see, I'm sure you've never encountered anything like it before in your life ... Please don't touch the bodies—the *replicas* of the bodies, and of the victims who were alive still at the time of their discovery—they're made of marzipan and other similar gel-like materials, the curator explained. As you can imagine, reproduction on a one-to-one scale was no easy feat, but in order to make the horror of the past *come alive*, or, more precisely—pardon me if I tend to get a bit overenthusiastic about it—to make the *fascination* of the horror *traversable*: for this, for us, there was no obstacle too great, *history as the setting for experience*, experience as traversable history, as I think I mentioned yesterday. Of course, the condition of the originals on which our reproductions are based was uniquely suited to our means of production; working with marzipan and similar materials requires a very delicate touch, a filigreed technique ... Naturally we've had to incorporate preservatives, but your standard wax figures these are not.—This is borderline outrageous, I thought; the replicas were so finely worked that you could make out every kneecap, every rib, every little bone, and the expression in those sunken eyes, unbelievable—and the *precision*! Though what I said aloud was: Marzipan? You made these out of *marzipan*? That can't be true!—I expected such an objection, the curator replied, suddenly annoyed, but what *is* can *never* be true! What sort of material should we have used, what rendering of the circumstances would you have found more agreeable? Plaster? Papier-mâché? Or how about *real* corpses, or actors *playing* corpses? Celluloid? Paper? Or would you have preferred something more abstract, what about simply *nothing at all*—air, void, smoke from a chimney? Or what about something carved from stone, or from granite perhaps, an antifascist statue, like the kind you find all over, in front of schools or police stations or at freeway interchanges; or what about something distorted *beyond all recognition*?! the curator irrupted in bitterness.—No distortion should exceed the point of recognition, there are limits, I heard a voice, the voice of one Schmidt, speaking from out of my own mouth, that's sacrilege, a crime against history!—What's a crime against history, the originals or the copies? the curator shot back nastily, only to admit, calmer now and conciliatory: Naturally, or rather, *by nature*, the concentration camp has not lost anything in transposition to the museum; by nature—nature and history, *natural history*, that's what concerns us here, isn't it?—by nature would be the only way of reconstructing recent German history, an *extreme vacation at the concentration camp*, but does this therefore mean that we need to live through everything all over again, history as repetition of the very same? You will have learned decades ago that's exactly what the dialectic forbids, and if you'll allow me, what we have here is repetition *by other means*; so what are you getting so worked up about? Furthermore, I'm dealing with a higher calling here, I'm fulfilling, as it were—and yes I'm aware of the gravity of the word—my duty ... to explain to you what I mean by duty; and I would now appreciate the opportunity to continue, without any further interjections from you, my tour, my recitation. As you've seen—no hard feelings between us, right? The curator laughed as he asked it—as you've seen, then, this is no conventional museum, and for that reason we have an interest in working not only with video installations but in conveying history, if you'll allow me, as *culinarily* as possible, and in order that we don't lack for *food for thought*, we've created these *space-within-a-space installations* ... Since the beginning we've been pioneers in the manufacture of space-within-a-space installations ... In the space-within-a-space installation sector we enjoy a worldwide reputation, the curator proudly explained, only then to add with a laugh: Since, though, German history would be unthinkable without the Austrians, we have invited three Viennese artists—Heller, Hollein, and Proksch—to design our horror installation, which they've given the cryptic title "*Arbeit macht frei, Arbeit macht reich.*" All in all, a very handsome piece of work ... It was the Austrians, by the way, who came up with the idea of using garden gnomes to portray the overseers—here, look, and there, and up there, in the watchtower, and over there too—that gnome's dressed up like Oliver Tobias in *The Stud* and that one as Eisenstein's *Ivan the Terrible* ... You guys really hit the mark with that one, I said, the brutality in those features is really dead on ... Dead on, huh? the curator replied and, after a pause: Since you brought it up ... would you like to move on to the next installation and take part in the execution of a partisan? Every shot hits its mark, this is history at close range, the Führer laughed, another absolutely incredible installation that truly incorporates the viewer ... Maybe in a while, I replied evasively, it's terribly hot in here. Yes, hot it is, the Führer confirmed, but it's always hot in here. Let's move on, then, to the toy and eyeglass collections.—Here you can see, that's understating it, here you can *experience* the warehouses of Auschwitz, here is the doll storeroom, across the way the eyeglass warehouse; unfortunately we've had to do without a reproduction of the gold-filling collection, the cost of securing it would have been prohibitive. With the money we saved there, though, we were for the most part able to acquire originals for both the doll and the eyeglass collections, I don't know if you can tell the difference. My God, these piles, these *masses*, I said, wiping the sweat from my forehead. Yes, the curator replied, the Germans have always had a feel for aggregate forms, for hoards, earthworks, piles, and lumps, such that one could speak of a real *mass culture*. And one *must*, I added. And one must, you're exactly right, the curator agreed. Yes, *by the way*, as the English say—and historically speaking, the English are Germans as well—come along, I'll show you one of the gems of our collection, we'll have a look at a Germanic estate in the pre-Christian era, a Germanic homestead ... And already another hall had materialized around us—it's amazing how quickly the scene can change!—in which smoke rose contentedly from little cottages whose thatched roofs grazed the ground, and women in long robes reclined on benches, staring off into the distance. So, what do you think? "A day in the life of a Germanic woman," a *historical* space-within-a-space installation, likely dating back to around 1938–39, there's still some dispute about it among archaeologists. But you see, even back then, back in the Stone Age, they embraced the idea of a traversable history, just like Rogner and we do today. Do you see the megalithic tomb in the distance? Now then, let's make ourselves at home in the prehistoric era, said the curator as he lead me over to a cottage. Let's have a look through the window into the interior, into a Germanic sitting room circa 1200 BC. You see, everything is in its place, the kettle over the hearth, the artfully lathed chairs around the table, the pottery on the shelf, the horn mounted on the crossbeam. A young woman came out of the door, clad in a cowl like a Franciscan monk, a raffia basket balanced on her hip. Pay attention, whispered my companion, and aloud he asked the woman her name. Edelberga, she replied. How many of you are there, was the curator's next question. Seven brothers and one sister, Edelberga replied in flawless German. And what are you doing right now? I'm just now leaving my lucent empire, if you are familiar with the reference, explained the Lady Edelberga, leaving the storehouse where my culinary and medicinal herbs are hung to dry, my thyme and arnica, eyebright and gypsyweed, and I am going now to the open hearth. Later I will assist my mother, a peasant wife, in scoring the fresh-baked loaves with our sacred symbol, the sun cross.—That's horseshit, I explode, the *sun cross*?! Nobody ever scored a sun cross on the bread—fertility and wheat! the symbol on the bread was always and *unmistakably* a vulva, a pubic triangle if you prefer, I know this from my great aunt, who of course had no idea herself of the significance, but even so, *that* is the symbol that's scored in the bread; and as for arnica and eyebright, they make no sense in a context like this, I know because I collect them myself up in the High Tauerns— But before the curator could intervene to pacify me—how rude my behavior must have seemed to the Lady Edelberga—dogs began barking and the sound of hooves came pounding nearer. From far-off, from out of the haze riders were emerging, draped in splendid, billowing cloaks, strapped with lavishly jeweled belts, their swords at their sides, lances in hand. Hark now, my brothers, I must put the roast in the fire and mix the draught! the lady cried and ran back to the hut without saying good-bye. Astonishing, isn't it, the Führer said as he continued on ahead of me, all that goes into a day's work for our ancestors in a historical space-within-a-space installation that was built back in 1938–39 . . . They dwelled peaceably and begat children, he suddenly began declaiming, and these were called Hölder, Hausmann and Schmied, Bauer, Pflüger, Bonde, Steilbart, Breit, Garbenbart, Bursch, Degen, Mann.

(. . .)

Here in these halls we house our Miscellaneous collection, the curator explains—how long now have we been underway? hours, days, *weeks?*—but even these scattered, apparently haphazard installations and performances have a certain charm of their own and offer a good overall view of our history and culture. Somewhere around here is the *German Chess Piece Carving Championships* of 1935, a forgotten discipline today, or take a look at that very naturalistic performance over there — unfortunately we're not allowed any closer, a respectable distance must be maintained, but you ought to be able to see well enough from here, can you see? — this performance represents the *Spring of Life*, or *Pure-blooded Mothers at Breeding*, done *a tergo*, like livestock, can you see? And can you see the uniformed man there holding a clipboard? That's the Head Inseminator . . . — And here we have a bar scene from Münster, a Sunday morning beer and schnapps, they just finished singing that old drinking song, *Three Cheers for Medical Orderly Neumann* — did you hear it? — and now the barkeep's saying — do you hear? — now the barkeep's saying: *Only war will show you what a man's really made of.* The barkeep's name is Heinz, by the way. — Now a similar scene, albeit from a ways further south, this installation is called *Ghost Story Hour at the Manor House Tavern*, also a very cozy atmosphere, right now a story's being told about a certain Globotschnigg, and one Lerch from Klagenfurt . . . You look tired, the Führer says suddenly. I am tired, I answer. That's too bad, says the Führer, without inquiring further, since you'll need to muster all your strength now, we're nearing another of the museum's highlights, a multimedia installation that brilliantly exploits all available means in a breathtaking *trompe les sens.* — Do you feel how cold it's become all of a sudden? Do you hear the storm and the music of the spheres? Jolyon Brettingham Smith composed it, but the name will mean nothing to you . . . Do you see the flag up on the summit? Have you noticed that no path leads past this installation? You're going to have to be steadfast and sure-footed now, the Führer laughs, since now we're climbing the highest mountain in the entire German Empire, *Großglockner*; yes, we find ourselves at last at the crux of our journey, on the narrow ridge between Kleinglockner and Großglockner . . . Do you see the ice ruts, how they cut dizzying vertical paths in the rock face to the left and right of us—I hope you don't suffer from vertigo, do you? Yes, a man may stray from the path of virtue and remain unscathed, but from this narrow ridge ... By the way, this time I haven't bothered with rope for you, I understand you don't like climbing with rope, is that right? The alpine guides will just haul you off into darkness and ruin if you climb with rope, isn't that so? I believe I read something to that effect a while back. Correct me please if I'm wrong, but careful now, one foot in front of the other, don't lose your balance, don't stumble, don't fall ...! *Onward now!* No! I shout, because suddenly an inexplicable weakness seizes me, as it has once before while climbing Großelend, and I'm afraid I'm not going to be able to hold myself upright this time. No, please, let's call it a day.—In here, the tour guide replied, I'm the one who gets to decide when enough is enough, and I say: Onward! Can't you see, a snowstorm's coming? It's either go on or collapse, there's no other option, there's no going back, no way around it. And since you're so passionate about traveling to Germany and experiencing things, piped the Führer, let's get on with it, and *bon courage, bon appétit,* here your hunger for experience will be sated, here your curiosity satisfied. Onward—or else I'll give you an experience you'll not soon forget ...!—But Großglockner belongs to *us,* I shouted, my voice growing weaker—not in the Museum of German History, not in any setting for experience, not in traversable, and even less in *surmountable* history ...! The Führer burst out laughing, he's convulsing with laughter. What did I tell you my name was, Kadritzke or Kurnitzky or was it Schmidt, my name is Schmidt, I'm here for the rent, was that it—? Ha ha, that's good, Kadritzke, Kurnitzky, Schmidt, and you believed me, I have to hand it to myself, I'm pleased at how well that turned out. But listen up and I'll tell you who you're actually dealing with: my name is Reiser, as I recall I've read before, and my anger is still not abated—Tobias Reiser, with a long *i* and a voiced *s*, sharp, as in *rousing*, just like the *rise* I'm getting out of you, do you understand? To put it another way, to put an end to all this: You may take your excursions into the profound, travel into the depths, but you'll never rise from the abyss I'll drive you to . . .!

Let's get this over with, then! I shouted with the last of my strength and pounced on my tormentor so that both of us lost our footing and plunged headlong into the abyss only to land on the museum floor; glass shattered, a projection screen tore, equipment that had been hidden from view fell down around us, the storm cut out, and the music of the spheres that I'd forgotten about in the meantime whined to a stop. What are you doing, have you gone mad? the curator screamed and picked himself back up. You're destroying the installation! Throw away that whip or I'll eat you, I wheezed, clutching his legs in my arms. Oh, so now you're quoting Kafka? the curator shouted, are you completely out of your mind?! Just look what you've done, this priceless installation . . .! —Installation? I asked in a daze and looked around: We must both have fallen, since shards lay all around. I beg your pardon, I said, I was lost in thought, I had a terrible daydream, maybe it was the alcohol . . . But whatever it was, I continued as I got back on my feet, one thing's for sure: You can't mock nature and get away with it . . .! Nor can you with history, the curator rejoined as if calling it even. Then I said: Who's mocking history? And he replied: Who's mocking nature? — Fine, I went on, let's just move on, shall we? I'm sure you've got a lot left to show me, there's bound to be more to German history than what I've seen — excuse me, than what I've *experienced* thus far . . . My attack, my episode just now — do you remember? — it gives me an idea, a fantastic idea; to put it culinarily, it's given me a taste for the demolition of space-within-a-space installations, that could be fun, really fun actually, *it could be art*, don't you think, *the destruction of the destruction*, a philosophical kind of pleasure . . . In that case you'll have to destroy reality itself, the curator countered, since — and take it from a man who holds degrees in History, Architecture, *and* Comparative Religion — the whole world, *all there is*, is only space installed within other space: history, reality, the universe, the cups in your cupboard, the dagger up your sleeve, the sword in the sheath, the penis — all only spaces installed in other spaces ... History in the museum, the museum throughout history, German troops in Poland, Allied forces in Germany, the space station in outer space — *outer space*, are you listening? — space-within-a-space installations. What's more, I dare say, but this stays between us — the curator brought his mouth very close to my ear and whispered — I dare say: the space-within-a-space installation is the secret of the cosmos itself.

It's midnight. I write: Rain beats against my brain. In front of me, the tour guide. Behind me, the tourist. No, I am the tourist. Another way, behind me the tour guide, in front of me the tourist. That's not it either, the tour guide's gone missing. In front of me, then, the tourist. Does he know the way? I wonder, since an inexplicable weakness seizes me, as it has once before while climbing Großelend, my strength's giving way and I can't go on. Granted, it was well before dawn when we set out, we've been underway for a while now, I'm not all that adept at navigating this icy and treacherous terrain, and still I'm baffled, *bothered* in fact by this fatigue; little as I like to admit it, it's true. (True? Who said that? Schmidt? Vollmer? The truth is only what we *take* it to be, that is the truth, Mr. Schmidt.) Let's call an end to this dangerous beginning, I say to the tourist, I want to turn back, here and now. — It's too late to turn back, replies the tourist, if the tourist it is, it's already after midnight. What one begins one must also bring to a finish — so enough then, not another word, enough.

Notes

p. 5   *Florian Köll*: architect and first caretaker of the Sudetendeutsche Hütte (here called the Prague Lodge); mayor of the parish of Windisch-Matrei (pop. approx. 5,000) 1974–89

p. 9   *Platterhof Hotel*: popular with Nazi officials and dignitaries; damaged in the Allied air raids in WWII

p. 10   *Gustav Ucicky*: purported to be an out-of-wedlock child of Gustav Klimt; directed the 1944 film *Das Herz muß schweigen* (The Heart Keeps Silent) and the 1960 film *Das Erbe von Björndal* (The Inheritance of Björndal)

p. 12   *"our own chancellor . . ."*: Franz Vranitzky, Social Democrat; left the private banking sector for the Ministry of Finance in 1984; appointed chancellor 1986 by Kurt Waldheim

p. 12   *"Frau von Damm—Helene"*: born in Ulmersfeld, Austria; married an American GI and emigrated to California; worked on Reagan's gubernatorial and presidential campaigns; served as ambassador to Austria 1983–85; married to Peter Gürtler, owner of the Hotel Sacher, 1985–86

p. 13   *Johannes Mario Simmel*: Austrian novelist and screenwriter; derided in the literary press as "kitsch" or as "opium for the masses"

p. 13   *"(reckless artistic nature, indeed!)"*: "Unbekümmerte Künstlernatur," poem by Erich Friend, Austrian poet, writer, and translator

p. 15   *Robert Rogner:* known for fantastical luxury hotels and resorts, including Rogner Hotel Europapark and Rogner Bad
Blumau

p. 20   *"To him* who wanders this street full of grievance, *I call out":*
"Der welcher wandert diese Straße voll Beschwerden," *The
Magic Flute,* Act II, Scene VII

p. 21   *Peter Turrini:* critically esteemed Austrian novelist, author
of the novel *Erlebnisse in der Mundhöhle* (Adventures in the
Oral Cavity)

p. 21   *Mario Ferrari-Brunnenfeld:* Austrian politician with the right-
wing populist Freedom Party of Austria

p. 24   *"late-born generation":* the generation born in the years following the end of WWII, including Kofler, b. 1947

p. 24   *"Yet where danger lies/Grows that which saves":* Friedrich
Hölderlin, "Patmos," trans. Richard Sieburth

p. 27   *"my name is Schmidt":* Alfred Paul Schmidt, Austrian crime
novelist who also wrote for the long running television cop
series *Tatort* (Scene of the Crime); also Alfred Schmidt, German citizen taken hostage by Hezbollah in 1987, with Rudolf Cordes

p. 27   *"An industrial banker name of Schiesser . . . it's Traub this time,*
Lackschuh-Traub": Horst Schiesser, businessman involved
in a 1986 financial scandal; Wolfgang Antes, conservative
Berlin politician, center of 1985 bribery and corruption
scandal; Wolfgang Albert Waldemar Schwanz, alias Otto
Schwanz, known sex-trafficker charged with counterfeiting
in the Antes Affair; Dietmar "Lackschuh" Traub ran a bor-
dello in Hamburg, and was murdered by the "St. Pauli Killer," Werner Pinzner

p. 28 "... *self-nominated* outpost-German ... *no Haider, no matter his first name*": Jörg Haider, chairman of the populist, right-extremist Freedom Party of Austria 1986–2000; "outpost German" designates a person living outside the German state and claiming German heritage who desires pan-Germanic unification

p. 30 *Systemzeit*: the Nazi designation for the Weimar Era, the "system" referred to being the Weimar Constitution

p. 30 "*this fellow Lerch*": Ernst Lerch, high-ranking Austrian Nazi; his father ran Café Lerch, a gathering place for Nazis prior to the Anschluss

p. 30 *Odilo Globocnik*: nickname "Globe," alt. spelling "Globotschnigg"; high-ranking Austrian Nazi, key figure in Operation Reinhard; the industrialized murder methods employed at concentration camps in the east have been attributed to him

p. 30 *Ernst Kaltenbrunner*: Austrian Nazi, senior SS officer

p. 31 "*that bastard Kreisky*": Bruno Kreisky, Social Democrat, Austrian politician of Jewish decent; sought asylum in Sweden during the war years; chancellor 1970–1983

p. 33 *Karl Roßmann*: the narrator of Kafka's *Amerika/The Man Who Disappeared*

p. 36 "*All these words belong to the estate of Kaspar of Ohlsdorf...*": in other words, Thomas Bernhard, who lived and worked in rural Ohlsdorf in Upper Austria

p. 37 "*The Treuchtlingers are the ablest painters...*": Ludwig Fels, self-styled writer of the working class and contemporary of Kofler's, apprenticed as a house painter in Treuchtlingen in his youth

p. 42 *"Labor Minister Hierl and Defense Contract Herr Oetker are expecting you!"*: Konstantin Hierl, Nazi bureaucrat in charge of the Reich Labor Service; Rudolf August Oetker, private sector entrepreneur, supported the Nazi government and profited in return

p. 43 *"Franz Mai's reign of terror"*: director of public broadcasting in the state of Saarland when it was made a part of the Federal Republic in 1957; this "reign" was marked by controversies concerning administrative appointments and the sale of on-air advertising

p. 44 *"smoking dope from Thailand . . . any better than Hans Albers has already done"*: *Dope*, a 1932 film directed by Kurt Gerron, starring Hans Albers

p. 45 *"I, Chinese Fritz, or I, Mister Joe . . . your friends Wilfrid Schulz and Renate"*: "Chinese" Fritz Schroer and "Mister Joe" were both victims of the St. Pauli Killer; Wilfrid Schulz was known as the "godfather" of the St. Pauli district; the name of his girlfriend Renate appears in court records of the period

p. 55 *". . . sitting there eclipsed beneath his waterfall gloom . . . Another B., this one a Burger . . ."*: Hermann Burger, Swiss writer, won the 1985 Ingeborg Bachmann prize for his story "The Waterfall-eclipse of Bad Gastein"; considered a meticulous prose stylist

p. 63 *". . . the fearsome Reger . . . my dear Atzbacher . . ."*: from Thomas Bernhard's *Old Masters*

p. 64 *"there are those who would like to be very technical . . . that freedom does not reign"*: Erich Fried famously asserted in a public speech, "Whoever says, here freedom reigns, he is lying, because freedom does not reign"

p. 72 *Professor Bornemann*: German crime writer and sexologist

p. 74 "*... actors Jaggberg, Janisch, and Herz-Kestranek ... detectives Hirth, Fichtl, and Schulz*": Austrian actors Kurt Jaggberg and Michael Janisch played Inspectors Hirth and Fichtl on the long-running cop drama *Tatort* (Scene of the Crime); Swiss actor Miguel Herz-Kestranik played Inspector Ullmann

p. 74 "*the arms dealer Proksch*": Udo Proksch, an Austrian businessman convicted of murder after conspiring to sink the cargo ship *Lucona*; the planned insurance fraud resulted in the death of six individuals; several federal ministers were also convicted for their involvement

p. 74 "*I go by Cordes, or Korbes*": Rudolf Cordes, West German businessman taken hostage by Hezbollah in 1987; "Herr Korbes" is a story from the Brothers Grimm

p. 76 *Rolf Torring*: The hero of a series of young adult adventure stories, *The Rolf Torring Adventures,* originally published 1930–39 and promoting the imperial and racist ideologies of the day; the series continued to be printed after the war, with appropriately adapted content

p. 76 "*A real* Leo Frank *thriller*": Leo Frank, Austrian crime writer and journalist, former criminal investigator; covered the Eichmann trial in Israel; wrote several episodes for the television series *Tatort* (Scene of the Crime)

p. 76 "Alles klar, Herr Kommissar": ("Got that, Commissioner?") Leo Frank's 1970s radio show; Falco's 1982 hit song

p. 77 *Red Zora*: protagonist of an anarchist children's book, *Rote Zora und ihre Bande* (The Outsiders of Uskoken Castle), by Kurt Held, 1941, and adapted as a television miniseries in

1979; likewise the name taken by a feminist guerrilla group in Germany, 1977–95

p. 77   *The White Rose*: nonviolent student resistance organization in Nazi Germany

p. 77   *"You mean* Stinkhorn? *. . . she got iced, says Flounder"*: with reference to *Der Butt* (The Flounder) by Günter Grass, "Kein Neid auf die Stinkmorchel mehr"

p. 78   *"Asscheek Eddy"*: "Arschbacken-Ede" or "Hasch Eddy" or "Klunker-Kutte"; a criminal informer in the Antes Affair

p. 83   *Gruppenführer*: paramilitary rank in the Nazi party

p. 84   *"in the jungle of the cities"*: title of a Bertolt Brecht play, *Im Dickicht der Städte*, 1923

p. 85   *"Peter Lorenz: That's what they've made of him"*: conservative German politician, kidnapped by the terrorist group Movement 2 June; headline run in *Bild-Zeitung*, January 1975 over a front-page photo of the prisoner

p. 85   *Heinz Konsalik*: German novelist

p. 85   *Andrei Sakharov*: Russian nuclear scientist who spoke out strongly against the military application of nuclear technology; exiled within the USSR; intellectual freedom and disarmament movements rallied around his case

p. 85   "Why Schleyer Must Die": politically connected German businessman Hanns Martin Schleyer, former SS member, kidnapped and murdered by the Red Army Faction

p. 85 *Julius Hackethal*: outspoken German doctor whose views on alternative cancer therapies and assisted suicide provoked controversy

p. 89 *"Mortals live by labor and wage"*: Friedrich Hölderlin, "Evening Fantasy," trans. Scott Horton

p. 92 *Branko*: character from Kurt Held's 1941 *Rote Zora und ihre Bande* (The Outsiders of Uskoken Castle)

p. 92 *Have you read me as Nagl, in* Winterreise?: the protagonist and title of a 1978 novel by Gerhard Roth

p. 104 *Utta Danella, Heinz Konsalik*: best-selling German authors of light, popular fiction

p. 104 *Helsinki baskets*: the agenda for the Helsinki Accords—signed in 1975 by all the countries of Europe (save Albania), as well as the United States and Canada—consisted of four primary topics, or "baskets"

p. 107 *"He that understands and does not act has not understood"*: Bruno Manser, environmentalist and indigenous rights activist, missing and presumed dead

p. 107 *"Teufel and Langhans of Kommune 1"*: Fritz Teufel and Rainer Langhans, of the New Left, influenced by Maoism and psychoanalysis, established the living experiment Kommune 1 to challenge fascism and bourgeois norms

p. 107 *"The long march through the institutions"*: Rudi Dutschke, activist in the German Student Movement of the 1960s, advocated a long march through the institutions of power ("Der lange Marsch durch die Institutionen") to change the machinery from within

p. 107 *"The* great refusal"*: Herbert Marcuse, *One-Dimensional Man*, 1964

p. 108 *"the . . .* Tupamaros"*: Uruguayan paramilitary guerrilla group

p. 110 *"this President of ours"*: Kurt Waldheim, conservative Christian President of Austria, 1986–1992, whose rank and involvement with the Wehrmacht during WWII—omitted from his autobiography—were revealed during his run for presidency; the ensuing scandal became known as the Waldheim Affair

p. 113 *"I, Lenz"*: Jakob Michael Reinhold Lenz, German poet, 1751–1792; likewise the protagonist of Georg Büchner's innovative and unfinished novella *Lenz*, which fictionalizes the records of the factual Lenz's descent into apparent madness

p. 115 *"the Nature Theater of Oklahoma"*: Kafka, *Amerika / The Man Who Disappeared*

p. 116 *"He gave his name as Kurnitzky"*: Horst Kurnitzky, b. 1938, German philosopher, architect, and religious scholar

p. 126 *"three Viennese artists—Heller, Hollein, and Proksch"*: Artist, poet, singer, actor André Heller; architect and designer Hans Hollein; businessman and felon Udo Proksch

p. 130 *Ulf Kadritzke*: German Marxist sociologist, b. 1943

WERNER KOFLER (1947–2011) was born in Carinthia, Austria, and died in Vienna. He studied to be a teacher before turning to writing, publishing numerous novels and plays. His awards include the Arno-Schmidt-Stipendium in 1996 and the Buch.Preis in 2004.

LAUREN K. WOLFE studied writing at the School of the Art Institute of Chicago and now studies Comparative Literature at New York University.

MICHAL AJVAZ, *The Golden Age.*
The Other City.
PIERRE ALBERT-BIROT, *Grabinoulor.*
YUZ ALESHKOVSKY, *Kangaroo.*
FELIPE ALFAU, *Chromos.*
Locos.
IVAN ÂNGELO, *The Celebration.*
The Tower of Glass.
ANTÓNIO LOBO ANTUNES, *Knowledge of Hell.*
The Splendor of Portugal.
ALAIN ARIAS-MISSON, *Theatre of Incest.*
ROBERT ASHLEY, *Perfect Lives.*
GABRIELA AVIGUR-ROTEM, *Heatwave and Crazy Birds.*
DJUNA BARNES, *Ladies Almanack.*
Ryder.
MIQUEL BAUÇÀ, *The Siege in the Room.*
RENÉ BELLETTO, *Dying.*
MAREK BIENCZYK, *Transparency.*
ANDREI BITOV, *Pushkin House.*
ANDREJ BLATNIK, *You Do Understand.*
Law of Desire.
LOUIS PAUL BOON, *Chapel Road.*
My Little War.
Summer in Termuren.
ROGER BOYLAN, *Killoyle.*
IGNÁCIO DE LOYOLA BRANDÃO, *Anonymous Celebrity.*
Zero.
BONNIE BREMSER, *Troia: Mexican Memoirs.*
CHRISTINE BROOKE-ROSE, *Amalgamemnon.*
BRIGID BROPHY, *In Transit.*
The Prancing Novelist.
GABRIELLE BURTON, *Heartbreak Hotel.*
MICHEL BUTOR, *Degrees.*
Mobile.
G. CABRERA INFANTE, *Infante's Inferno.*
Three Trapped Tigers.
JULIETA CAMPOS, *The Fear of Losing Eurydice.*
ANNE CARSON, *Eros the Bittersweet.*

ORLY CASTEL-BLOOM, *Dolly City.*
LOUIS-FERDINAND CÉLINE, *North.*
Conversations with Professor Y.
London Bridge.
MARIE CHAIX, *The Laurels of Lake Constance.*
HUGO CHARTERIS, *The Tide Is Right.*
ERIC CHEVILLARD, *Demolishing Nisard.*
The Author and Me.
MARC CHOLODENKO, *Mordechai Schamz.*
JOSHUA COHEN, *Witz.*
EMILY HOLMES COLEMAN, *The Shutter of Snow.*
ERIC CHEVILLARD, *The Author and Me.*
ROBERT COOVER, *A Night at the Movies.*
ARIEL DORFMAN, *Konfidenz.*
ARKADII DRAGOMOSHCHENKO, *Dust.*
RIKKI DUCORNET, *Phosphor in Dreamland.*
The Complete Butcher's Tales.
The Jade Cabinet.
The Fountains of Neptune.
WILLIAM EASTLAKE, *The Bamboo Bed.*
Castle Keep.
Lyric of the Circle Heart.
JEAN ECHENOZ, *Chopin's Move.*
FRANÇOIS EMMANUEL, *Invitation to a Voyage.*
GUSTAVE FLAUBERT, *Bouvard and Pécuchet.*
MAX FRISCH, *I'm Not Stiller.*
Man in the Holocene.
CARLOS FUENTES, *Christopher Unborn.*
Distant Relations.
Terra Nostra.
Where the Air Is Clear.
GÉRARD GAVARRY, *Hoppla! 1 2 3.*
C. S. GISCOMBE, *Giscome Road.*
Here.
WITOLD GOMBROWICZ, *A Kind of Testament.*

FOR A FULL LIST OF PUBLICATIONS, VISIT: www.dalkeyarchive.com

JUAN GOYTISOLO, *Count Julian.*
Juan the Landless.
Makbara.
Marks of Identity.
JIŘÍ GRUŠA, *The Questionnaire.*
MELA HARTWIG, *Am I a Redundant Human Being?*
JOHN HAWKES, *The Passion Artist.*
Whistlejacket.
ELIZABETH HEIGHWAY, ED., *Contemporary Georgian Fiction.*
NAOYUKI II, *The Shadow of a Blue Cat.*
DRAGO JANČAR, *The Tree with No Name.*
GERT JONKE, *The Distant Sound.*
Homage to Czerny.
The System of Vienna.
MIEKO KANAI, *The Word Book.*
YORAM KANIUK, *Life on Sandpaper.*
ZURAB KARUMIDZE, *Dagny.*
DANILO KIŠ, *The Attic.*
The Lute and the Scars.
Psalm 44.
A Tomb for Boris Davidovich.
ANITA KONKKA, *A Fool's Paradise.*
GEORGE KONRÁD, *The City Builder.*
TADEUSZ KONWICKI, *A Minor Apocalypse.*
The Polish Complex.
ANNA KORDZAIA-SAMADASHVILI, *Me, Margarita.*
ELAINE KRAF, *The Princess of 72nd Street.*
JIM KRUSOE, *Iceland.*
AYSE KULIN, *Farewell: A Mansion in Occupied Istanbul.*
EMILIO LASCANO TEGUI, *On Elegance While Sleeping.*
VIOLETTE LEDUC, *La Bâtarde.*
EDOUARD LEVÉ, *Autoportrait.*
Newspaper.
Suicide.
Works.
MARIO LEVI, *Istanbul Was a Fairy Tale.*
ROSA LIKSOM, *Dark Paradise.*
FLORIAN LIPUŠ, *The Errors of Young Tjaž.*

YURI LOTMAN, *Non-Memoirs.*
MINA LOY, *Stories and Essays of Mina Loy.*
MICHELINE AHARONIAN MARCOM, *A Brief History of Yes.*
The Mirror in the Well.
DAVID MARKSON, *Reader's Block.*
Wittgenstein's Mistress.
CAROLE MASO, *AVA.*
HISAKI MATSUURA, *Triangle.*
ABDELWAHAB MEDDEB, *Talismano.*
GERHARD MEIER, *Isle of the Dead.*
HERMAN MELVILLE, *The Confidence-Man.*
AMANDA MICHALOPOULOU, *I'd Like*
GERALD MURNANE, *Barley Patch.*
Inland.
YVES NAVARRE, *Our Share of Time.*
Sweet Tooth.
DOROTHY NELSON, *In Night's City.*
Tar and Feathers.
ESHKOL NEVO, *Homesick.*
WILFRIDO D. NOLLEDO, *But for the Lovers.*
FLANN O'BRIEN, *At Swim-Two-Birds.*
The Dalkey Archive.
The Poor Mouth.
The Third Policeman.
CLAUDE OLLIER, *The Mise-en-Scène.*
Wert and the Life Without End.
PATRIK OUŘEDNÍK, *Europeana.*
The Opportune Moment, 1855.
BORIS PAHOR, *Necropolis.*
FERNANDO DEL PASO, *News from the Empire.*
Palinuro of Mexico.
MANUEL PUIG, *Betrayed by Rita Hayworth.*
The Buenos Aires Affair.
Heartbreak Tango.
ANN QUIN, *Berg.*
Passages.
Three.
Tripticks.

ISHMAEL REED, *The Free-Lance Pallbearers.*
The Last Days of Louisiana Red.
Juice!
The Terrible Threes.
The Terrible Twos.
Yellow Back Radio Broke-Down.

JOÃO UBALDO RIBEIRO, *House of the Fortunate Buddhas.*

RAINER MARIA RILKE, *The Notebooks of Malte Laurids Brigge.*

ALAIN ROBBE-GRILLET, *Project for a Revolution in New York.*
A Sentimental Novel.

AUGUSTO ROA BASTOS, *I the Supreme.*

DANIËL ROBBERECHTS, *Arriving in Avignon.*

ALIX CLEO ROUBAUD, *Alix's Journal.*

JACQUES ROUBAUD, *The Form of a City Changes Faster, Alas, Than the Human Heart.*
The Great Fire of London.
Hortense in Exile.
Hortense Is Abducted.
Some Thing Black.

RAYMOND ROUSSEL, *Impressions of Africa.*

VEDRANA RUDAN, *Night.*

TOMAŽ ŠALAMUN, *Soy Realidad.*

LYDIE SALVAYRE, *The Company of Ghosts.*
The Lecture.
The Power of Flies.

NATHALIE SARRAUTE, *Do You Hear Them?*
Martereau.
The Planetarium.

STIG SÆTERBAKKEN, *Siamese.*
Self-Control.
Through the Night.

ARNO SCHMIDT, *Collected Novellas.*
Collected Stories.
Nobodaddy's Children.
Two Novels.

GAIL SCOTT, *My Paris.*

VIKTOR SHKLOVSKY, *Bowstring.*
Literature and Cinematography.

Theory of Prose.
Third Factory.
Zoo, or Letters Not about Love.

PIERRE SINIAC, *The Collaborators.*

KJERSTI A. SKOMSVOLD, *The Faster I Walk, the Smaller I Am.*

JOSEF ŠKVORECKÝ, *The Engineer of Human Souls.*

GILBERT SORRENTINO, *Aberration of Starlight.*
Imaginative Qualities of Actual Things.
Mulligan Stew.
Steelwork.

GERTRUDE STEIN, *The Making of Americans.*
A Novel of Thank You.

GONÇALO M. TAVARES, *A Man: Klaus Klump.*
Jerusalem.
Learning to Pray in the Age of Technique.

DUMITRU TSEPENEAG, *Hotel Europa.*
The Necessary Marriage.
Pigeon Post.
Vain Art of the Fugue.

ESTHER TUSQUETS, *Stranded.*

DUBRAVKA UGRESIC, *Lend Me Your Character.*
Thank You for Not Reading.

TOR ULVEN, *Replacement.*

MATI UNT, *Brecht at Night.*
Diary of a Blood Donor.
Things in the Night.

LUISA VALENZUELA, *Dark Desires and the Others.*
He Who Searches.

LLORENÇ VILLALONGA, *The Dolls' Room.*

DIANE WILLIAMS, *Excitability: Selected Stories.*
Romancer Erector..

MARGUERITE YOUNG, *Angel in the Forest.*
Miss MacIntosh, My Darling

AND MORE ...